The North Carolina State Ports Authority

The North Carolina State Ports Authority

Charles E. Landon

Duke University Press   Durham, N. C.   1963

Preface

Created in 1945 by an act of the General Assembly, the North Carolina State Ports Authority was assigned the task of constructing and operating modern ocean terminals to aid the economic development of the state. Such terminals, later enlarged, were opened for use in 1952 at Morehead City and Wilmington.

The purpose of this study is to investigate and give an account of the administrative, political, and economic activities and problems of the Authority. In so doing I have attempted to indicate the degree of success the Authority has attained in realizing its objectives during a decade of operations.

I wish to thank the Ford Foundation for grants of funds that provided the time for conducting the research on this project, and the Duke University Council on Research for a grant of funds that made publication of the study possible. Appreciation is expressed also for the aid and information provided by L. C. Bruce, Jr., Director of Public Relations; Ruff A. DeVane, Secretary-Treasurer; and E. E. Lee, Jr., Director of Commerce and Traffic, of the administrative staff of the State Ports Authority. I wish to express gratitude also to Professor Marvin L. Fair of the School of Business Administration, The American University, for valuable suggestions concerning the manuscript, and to Mrs. Elizabeth Caviness Levings of the North Carolina Department of Archives and History for making available the files of the State Ports Authority. Needless to say, any shortcomings in this book are solely my own responsibility.

CHARLES E. LANDON

Durham, North Carolina

Contents

Contents

Illustrations
    between pages 28-29

Tables

The North Carolina State Ports Authority

1. Background, Structure, and Organization of the North Carolina State Ports Authority

Background

The North Carolina State Ports Authority was created in 1945 by an act of the General Assembly of North Carolina[1] after more than a quarter of a century of agitation for state aid for port and harbor development. Agitation began in the early 1920's during the administration of Governor Cameron Morrison, who saw a relationship between the growth of seaports and the development of the inland sections of the state. Governor Morrison led the movement for the approval of a state bond issue of $8,500,000 for the development of state ports. The bond issue was defeated in a special election in November, 1924, the result, it is said, of the inability of voters in the Piedmont and western sections of the state to realize the importance of seaports to the development of the entire state.

The function of the State Ports Authority as brought up to date in 1953 by a later law of the General Assembly is

to develop and improve the harbors or seaports at Wilmington, Morehead City, and Southport, and such other places including inland ports and facilities as may be deemed feasible for a more expeditious and efficient handling of water-borne commerce from and to any place or places in the State of North Carolina and other states and foreign countries. . . . And in general to do or perform any act or function which may tend or be useful toward the development and improvement of harbors, seaports and inland ports of the State of North Carolina and to increase the movement of water-borne commerce, foreign and domestic, to, through, and from said harbors and ports.[2]

There are no state-owned docks at Southport, but the legislation authorizes the State Ports Authority to develop such facilities if and when there is a recognized need. Although Southport is located near the open ocean and has one of the deepest (forty-foot) and roomiest

[1] H.B. 816; also Session Laws of North Carolina 1945, chap. 1097.
[2] Session Laws of North Carolina 1953, chap. 191.
(Other powers of the State Ports Authority are discussed later in chapters to which they are related.)

harbors on the South Atlantic coast, deep-water facilities are not feasible at present because there is no demand for deep-water services at the city or in its immediate hinterland. At present manufacturing industries show no interest in locating at Southport in spite of a daily supply of 42 million gallons of fresh water that gushes up in springs from an underground stream. In 1959 the voters of the state approved a contingency bond issue of $500,000 to enable port facilities to be developed at Southport if and when a sound opportunity should arise.

This legislation empowers the State Ports Authority to develop inland ports, but to date nothing has been done in this field. At a meeting in Raleigh in June, 1961, however, this organization expressed optimism over prospects for the development of an inland port at Fayetteville in Cumberland County. The municipal port there already handles about 400,000 tons of cargo a year, almost all of it being gasoline that is barged up the Cape Fear River from Wilmington. Recently the county commissioners of Cumberland County donated a large tract of land on the river at Fayetteville to the state for use in the future development of a river port.[3]

The act of the General Assembly creating the State Ports Authority had been preceded by other less inclusive acts. Both Morehead City and Wilmington had made efforts to improve their port facilities before the state was asked to provide aid. The Morehead City Port Commission was created in 1933 and the Wilmington Port Commission in 1935, both under authority granted by acts of the General Assembly.[4]

[3] *Durham Morning Herald,* June 28, 1961, A:2.

[4] Public-Local and Private Laws of North Carolina, Session 1933, chap. 75. Public-Local and Private Laws of North Carolina, Session 1935, chap. 390.

In 1935, the General Assembly also enacted legislation authorizing the City of Southport to establish a port commission. This act had provisions similar to the one providing for the Morehead City Port Commission. Although the act creating the State Ports Authority included Southport among the ports to be developed, that port has not been included in the plans of the State Ports Authority.

The following quotation from the law creating the Morehead City Port Commission indicates the prevailing thought regarding the development of the state's seaports. The law declared it "to be the policy of the State of North Carolina to promote, encourage, and develop water transportation service and facilities in connection with the commerce of the United States and to foster and preserve in full vigor both rail and water transportation, and that Morehead City, North Carolina is hereby declared to be a port to be developed in connection with the interior of the State of North Carolina necessary and desirable and in the public interest of the entire State that there shall be established through Morehead City through connecting water-and-rail rates in connection with shipping companies and other transportation companies and in accordance with the provisions of the acts of Congress in the United States and the laws of North Carolina" (Sec. 11).

In the case of Morehead City, funds for carrying out the purposes of the act were to be obtained by the issue of bonds or other securities which were to be sold to the Reconstruction Finance Corporation or other government agencies. The bonds were to be liquidated from the earnings of the port and, with the approval of the voters, a municipal levy on all taxable property not to exceed 10¢ per $100 of taxable values, if earnings were insufficient. In March, 1935, the General Assembly enacted legislation providing that if the Reconstruction Finance Corporation did advance a loan, the state, in addition to the security advanced by the Morehead City Port Commission, would pledge as security rentals of the state-owned Atlantic and North Carolina Railroad Company sufficient to guarantee any deficiency in the required annual payment to amortize the principal.[5] The state made this pledge because it was interested in enhancing the value of the railroad. The Port Commission was able to sell $326,000 in bonds to the Reconstruction Finance Corporation. The facilities provided under the legislation were to be both owned and operated by the Port Commission.

At Wilmington the Board of Commissioners of New Hanover County was empowered, with the approval of the voters, to levy and appropriate annually for six years the sum of 2¢ per $100 of the assessed valuation of taxable property to encourage the development of the port of Wilmington. The activities of the Wilmington Port Commission were confined to promotion and to informing the public about the port. No jurisdiction was given over the operation of the port or any of its activities.

The Wilmington Port Commission decided almost immediately that improved facilities were necessary if the port were to realize its maximum possibilities, and engineering plans were prepared for certain terminals and warehouses. In the search for funds, first an unsuccessful attempt was made in 1938 to obtain a loan from the Public Works Administration, then, early in 1941 a request to the Reconstruction Finance Corporation for a self-liquidating loan was refused. Later, in January, 1945, the Port Commission, supported by the officials of New Hanover County and the City of Wilmington, requested Governor R. Gregg Cherry to make state financial aid available, preferably through legislative appropriation, so planned con-

[5] Public Laws of North Carolina 1935, chap. 446.

struction could begin immediately at the end of the war. The estimated cost of the improvements was $900,000.[6]

Immediately the governor authorized the State Planning Board, an advisory agency, to make a thorough investigation of the proposal in order to determine whether or not, from the standpoint of the entire state, there would be economic justification for such aid. Inasmuch as the General Assembly was already in session, only a short time existed in which to make the study if proposals were to be submitted to the Assembly.

The State Planning Board obtained information from a variety of sources. It visited Wilmington to observe the port facilities there, drew on historical and current materials from state and federal sources, consulted a few specialists in transportation and economic geography, interviewed public officials of other states with experience in port development, and interviewed or corresponded with scores of shippers and their trade associations. The North Carolina Traffic League, comprised of almost all major shippers in the state, provided much valuable assistance and information. These shippers were asked in effect the following questions:

1. Would an improved port at Wilmington aid them as shippers?

2. Would they as citizens and taxpayers favor state aid for port development?

Information also was supplied on this point by copies of a survey made by the Wilmington Port Commission among the shippers of the state in 1943 in an attempt to obtain definite commitments of new traffic. This survey obtained commitments of approximately 360,000 tons, provided that adequate facilities and adequate steamship services would be available. In addition, 100,000 tons of potential new traffic was discovered, consisting of numerous commodities not using the port regularly at the time.

On the basis of the information collected, although not all of it favored port development, the State Planning Board recommended the appropriation of modest amounts for the purpose. Another factor which influenced the decision of this board was the possibility of heavy unemployment at Wilmington after the end of the war. The

[6] For more details, see "Report of Wilmington Port Development" to Governor R. Gregg Cherry, by the North Carolina State Planning Board, Felix A. Grisette, Managing Director, Feb. 27, 1945. Mimeographed.

city had undergone a marked expansion in population because of the locating there of a wartime federal shipbuilding yard.[7]

The late Rinaldo B. Page, publisher of the *Star* and *News* at Wilmington, generally is considered to be the father of the State Ports Authority. Mr. Page was an advocate of state support for deep-water facilities at both Morehead City and Wilmington. From the 1930's until his death in 1955 he assumed the responsibility of the state's first spokesman in behalf of a modern ports program and devoted the policy of his newspapers to a movement for better seaports and for returning the state to its former position in world commerce.

Mr. Page began a campaign for a State Ports Authority in the 1940's. Looking ahead to the construction of terminals, he obtained a long-term lease from the United States Maritime Commission for a section of the wartime shipbuilding yard at Wilmington. He also began negotiations with the Morehead City Port Commission for the facilities erected there in 1937. Further, he obtained a loan of $90,000 from the WPA to finance studies and surveys to determine the best type of terminals to build.[8]

Both Morehead City and Wilmington supported the movement, and later the port commissions in both ports took up the cause and it was on these efforts that the movement for a State Ports Authority was founded. Mr. Page was an original member of the Authority and he was elected its first chairman. Another citizen of Wilmington, the late Cyrus D. Hogue, Sr., an attorney and the chairman of the Wilmington Port Commission, prepared the legislation to create the State Ports Authority.[9]

Before 1900 the federal government and private industry were relied upon to develop seaports, and during the preceding half century the railroads were dominant in the development of the more important ocean and lake ports. But uncontrolled private development was found to be either objectionable or inadequate. The port authority

[7] *Ibid.*, introductory statement by Mr. Grisette.

[8] This information about Rinaldo B. Page is summarized from "R. B. Page and the Ports," by Al G. Dickson, Executive Director of the *Star* and *News*, in *North Carolina State Ports*, Fall, 1960, p. 5. *North Carolina State Ports* is the official publication of the State Ports Authority. It was first called *North Carolina Ports*, but beginning with the issue of Nov., 1954, the name was changed to *North Carolina State Ports*.

[9] *Ibid.*

is the answer to this problem.[10]   The port authority, usually an agency of the state, but often of the municipality and sometimes of more than a single state, is the modern method of "achieving enlightened, co-ordinated, and planned harbor, port, and trade promotion and opera-tion with protection to both public and private interests."[11]

All of the neighboring coastal states of North Carolina have port authorities.   The Savannah District Authority, a municipal body, was created by the General Assembly of Georgia in 1925.   It is now largely a promotional agency and traffic bureau.   In 1945 the General Assembly created the Georgia Ports Authority.   It was intended to implement rather than to supplant the Savannah District Authority. In 1942 the General Assembly of South Carolina created the South Carolina State Ports Authority.   The Norfolk Port Authority, a municipal agency, was created by the General Assembly of Virginia in 1948, and in 1952 that body created the Virginia State Ports Authority.

The main problem facing a port authority is the obtaining of funds for the provision of modern terminal facilities and harbor im-provements for handling general cargo.   Private enterprise usually owns and operates the facilities for handling bulk cargo but will not normally provide them for caring for general cargo.[12]

Structure and Organization

Originally, the State Ports Authority consisted of a board of seven members.   In 1949, during the administration of Governor W. Kerr Scott, it was enlarged to nine members, one of whom, the director of the Department of Conservation and Development, was a member ex officio.   Of the seven members of the original board, only three were reappointed and one of those resigned shortly after reappoint-ment.   All seven members resigned in March, 1949, in a spirit of co-operation in order to permit the governor to name new members of his own choosing.   Each member agreed to serve if reappointed.   In 1953, during the administration of Governor William B. Umstead, the board was reduced to seven members, and the director of the Board

---

[10] See M. L. Fair, *Port Administration in the United States* (Cambridge, Md., 1954), pp. 41-43.
[11] G. F. Mott, *A Survey of United States Ports* (New York, 1951), p. 30.
[12] *Ibid.,* p. 107.

of Conservation and Development was no longer a member ex officio.[13] Only two of the members appointed in 1949 were reappointed by Governor Umstead. The term of office of all the members of the board expired in the middle of 1957 during the administration of Governor Luther H. Hodges and he did not reappoint them because of dissatisfaction with the policies of the Authority. A new group of seven members took the oath of office in November, 1957.

In the original legislation board members were appointed for terms of six years, but in 1953 the terms were reduced to four years, which made them coincide with the term of office of the governor who, in North Carolina, cannot succeed himself. Each governor could then appoint the full board when he entered office. Such a policy violates the concept of a "port authority." The organization can be used for the purposes of political patronage, which does not assure capable and interested members of the board. When the terms of office overlap, the board always has experienced members to provide continuity for its activities. Of course, when a new governor has the power to appoint the entire board, he may reappoint some or all of the existing members, but such a practice is not assured. In the original legislation the terms were made to overlap. The three members from the port cities were appointed for six-year terms, two of the remaining members for three-year terms, and two for four-year terms. After that each appointee would serve six years.

The General Assembly of 1961 raised the membership of the board to nine, changed the term of office to six years, and made the terms overlapping as in the original legislation. Three members are to be appointed for two years each, three for four years each, and three for six years each. Thereafter all regular terms are for six years.[14]

The members of the board must be from the state at large and must be selected in a manner that fairly represents each section and all of the agricultural, industrial, and business interests. Table 1 shows the cities from which the members of the different boards have been selected. The first board is the only one on which the port cities have had representatives. The original law required that the county in which each of the three ports was situated should have a member

[13] For the different changes in the law, see H. B. 725, 1949 General Assembly, and S. B. 170, 1953 General Assembly; also, Session Laws of North Carolina 1949, chap. 892, and 1953, chap. 191.
[14] Session Laws of North Carolina 1961, chap. 143.

on the board. These were the members who were appointed for six-year terms.

A study of Table 1 will reveal that the central section of the state (roughly, the Piedmont section) has had the largest number of members on each of the boards, except for the board appointed in 1945, and the largest total number on the five boards combined. The eastern part of the state has had about two-thirds as many members as the central section on the five boards combined. The western section of the state has had only a few representatives.

Table 1. Cities Represented on Each Board of the State Ports Authority and Year of Appointment of Each Board[a]

First–1945	Second–1949	Third–1953	Fourth–1957	Fifth–1961
Fayetteville	Clinton	Charlotte	Asheville	Burlington
Gastonia	Durham	Gastonia	Chapel Hill	Greensboro
Morehead City	Edenton	Goldsboro	Durham[c]	Greenville
Morganton	Fayetteville	Hallsboro	Gastonia	McAdenville
Southport	Gastonia	Laurinburg	High Point	Pinehurst
Wilmington	Hallsboro	Lenoir	Kinston[c]	Raleigh
Winston-Salem	North Wilkesboro	Winston-Salem	Pinehurst	Robersonville
	Raleigh[b]		Roanoke Rapids	Tarboro
	Winston-Salem		Tarboro	Winston-Salem

[a] No account is taken of appointments on account of resignations.
[b] Ex officio.
[c] Appointed in 1959.

Four different persons have served as chairmen of the board. The first one, R. B. Page, served from 1945 until 1949. Next was A. G. Myers, financier and textile manufacturer of Gastonia, who served from 1949 until late in 1953. Mr. Myers was a member of the State Ports Authority for eight years and had an important part in pushing the original construction program. The third chairman was Edwin Pate, banker and executive of commercial fertilizer companies of Laurinburg, who held the office from late in 1953 until the fall of 1957. The present chairman, J. M. Reeves of Pinehurst, is Chairman of the Board of Reeves Brothers, Inc., of New York City. He was appointed by Governor Hodges in 1957 and reappointed by Governor Sanford in 1961.

The law required the State Ports Authority[15] to establish an office and on January 1, 1948, Wilmington was selected as its site. Gradual dissatisfaction with this site developed in Morehead City, and early in 1955 representatives from there asked that the office be moved to the

[15] Hereinafter the term "Authority" will be used for this organization except in instances where the full name seems to be more appropriate.

state capital, Raleigh, about 150 miles inland, or to another location, several of which were suggested.   One suggestion was that the office be located at some point in the Piedmont industrial area.   Interests in Morehead City believed that their city had not received the attention it deserved and that moving the office would remove the alleged pressure and influence from those in the office on the part of interests at Wilmington and would end the bickering between the two cities. A spokesman for the interests at Morehead City stated that his city had not received the solicitation in the tobacco area of the state that Wilmington had received in the textile area.[16]

The Authority decided, however, to keep its office at Wilmington, stating that it was interested in helping both ports as well as the best interest of the entire state.   It also believed that the office should be in one of the two port cities, and inasmuch as an investment had been made in the facilities at Wilmington, it was thought best to remain there.

Continued rivalry between the two ports, however, was the underlying reason for the refusal of Governor Hodges to reappoint the members of the board, whose term of office expired in 1957, and for the resignation of the executive director.   Interests at Morehead City felt that Wilmington was being favored to the detriment of their port. The executive director had stated that he did not want cutthroat competition between the ports and that the products most suited to each port would be shipped through it.   The complaints of interests at Morehead City may have had some basis, because correspondence in the files of the Authority in the State Department of Archives and History indicates friction between the executive director and the terminal manager at Morehead City, who resigned later.   Furthermore, in a letter to a prospective shipper the executive director said that "The Port of Morehead City from its very beginning has been a failure."   He pointed out that two different surveys had been made and that both of them definitely favored Wilmington.[17]

The beliefs of the interests at Morehead City were strengthened by the report of a survey made for the Authority by the New York firm of James C. Buckley, terminal and transportation consultants,

[16] *Durham Morning Herald,* April 24, 1955, 1:4.
[17] Richard S. Marr to John H. Frazier, Jr., President, P. R. Markley, Inc., Philadelphia, Pa., Jan. 6, 1958.

which recommended the development of Wilmington as the primary port, with Morehead City having a secondary status.

This report states that normally the trade would be handled in one port rather than in the two already established. On the basis of the resources of the hinterland in which each port has an advantage over or is equal to competing ports in terms of transportation cost, analysis disclosed that for most cargo the division of traffic would be 5 or 6 per cent to Morehead City and 94 or 95 per cent to Wilmington. For leaf tobacco the division would be 26 per cent to Morehead City and 74 per cent to Wilmington.[18]

To placate the interests at Morehead City, the new board, in December, 1957, ordered the moving of the executive offices to Raleigh. These offices are those of the executive director, the director of commerce and traffic, and the director of public relations. The general or administrative offices remain at Wilmington. Since the moving of the executive offices to Raleigh and the hiring of a new executive director, complaints from Morehead City have subsided. The new executive director, D. Leon Williams, who died on June 1, 1962, was careful to deal fairly with the two ports, and tried to develop each one along the lines of its best interests.

Although both state terminals handle several of the same commodities and although the policy of the Authority is to provide equal facilities for each port, the policy always has been to permit each port to specialize in the products it can handle the more advantageously.

When appointing the new members of the board in 1957, Governor Hodges outlined a five-point program. These points were (1) objectivity on the part of the board and the executive director by maintaining a state-wide perspective, (2) better public relations in selling the ports to shipping lines and to North Carolina industry and business, (3) an end to inter-port squabbling, (4) increased tonnages, and (5) a long-range program for development of the ports.[19]

The board elects a member to serve as chairman and one to serve as vice-chairman, as well as a secretary-treasurer who may not neces-

---

[18] James C. Buckley, Inc., Terminal and Transportation Consultants, *A Development Study of North Carolina State Ports for the North Carolina State Ports Authority* (New York, 1957), p. 5. Hereinafter this report will be referred to as the Buckley Report.

[19] See an editorial in the *Greensboro Daily News*, Nov. 4, 1957; also *North Carolina State Ports*, Spring, 1958, pp. 2-5.

sarily be a member of the board.   A security bond is required for the treasurer, the cost of which is paid as a necessary expense of the Authority.   Members receive $7.00 a day when in performance of their duty, plus necessary expenses for travel.   Seven cents a mile is allowed for automobiles, and the actual fare by other transportation. The allowance for subsistence is the actual amount spent, but with an upper limit of $8.00 a day.[20]   Meetings are upon the call of the chairman, and a majority constitutes a quorum.   An executive committee is appointed with authority to act for the board as a whole in matters not already acted upon by the board.

The board appoints an executive director to administer and manage the development and operations of the state ports. He serves at the pleasure of the board, but his salary is fixed by the governor, with the approval of the Advisory Budget Commission of the state.   The director has the power to appoint, employ, and dismiss employees, but their compensation is fixed by the board.

The Authority has had three executive directors.   The first one served from January 1, 1948, until December 31, 1953, and the second from January 1, 1954, until December 31, 1957.   The first executive director had retired after long years of service in the United States Army Corps of Engineers, and thus possessed a type of knowledge that was advantageous in the early stages of port development. The second director had retired from the United States Army, in which he had gained wide experience in the types of activities associated with the construction and development of seaports.

The change in executive directors at the end of 1953 apparently was the result of dissatisfaction on the part of some of the members of the board who believed that the policies being followed would not soon attract the traffic required to make the state ports self-sustaining. The heavy investment had been made on the basis of their becoming self-supporting.   These members wished to have the ports developed, but did not want them to become a financial burden on the taxpayers. Consequently, they favored a program of aggressive solicitation of business.   The feeling was that the executive director did not have a well-geared promotional program and that he was not aggressive enough in trying to attract traffic to the terminals.[21]   Upon resigning, the executive director charged that "politics and petty jealousies"

[20] Session Laws of North Carolina 1953, chap. 1165, Sec. 4.
[21] Durham Morning Herald, Oct. 21, 1953, 1:4.

had influenced the board's action.[22]　Upon assuming office, the new executive director stated that the ports program was demoralized, and in some instances incompetent, and would have to be reorganized. He emphasized that development of the ports would require hard work and much traffic solicitation.[23]

In favor of the first executive director, it can be said that at first his task was not one of traffic development but one of port construction.　Under his direction the first and basic stage in the provision of fixed plant was completed, and a certain amount of promotional work was preliminary to this stage.　Until this construction was completed, the state terminals had no attraction for traffic.　But with this stage completed, it may be that the executive director was too much the engineer to develop the facilities commercially, a task that is more in the field of business management.　When the fixed plant has been provided, its managers can either wait for traffic to come to the port or they can go after the traffic.　The continuous practice of the latter policy seems to be necessary for these ports, in view of the competition and other problems facing them.

In the fall of 1957 complaints similar to those just mentioned convinced Governor Hodges that an entirely new board was necessary for a fresh start and different approach.　He was especially concerned about the selling job that was being done on shipping companies and North Carolina businessmen.　Consequently, the new membership of the board appointed at this time was selected with this problem in mind.　More of the members were from upstate communities than on previous boards, and none of them was from the port areas.　Also, in hiring a new executive director, it was emphasized that he should concentrate upon developing business and persuading shipping lines to make Wilmington and Morehead City ports of call.　This new executive director, who took office in February, 1958, had had many years of experience in operating similar facilities in Georgia.　After Mr. Williams' death in the summer of 1962, E. N. Richards, a member of the board, served as acting director.　On November 9, 1962, James W. Davis, director of planning of the Maryland Port Authority, was chosen to be the fourth executive director of the North Carolina State Ports Authority.　In early December, 1962, the board of directors

[22] *Ibid.*, 1:1.
[23] *Ibid.*, July 10, 1954, 1:8.

voted to construct a new office building in Wilmington and to return the executive offices from Raleigh to Wilmington.

M. L. Fair in his study of port administration found that, as of 1951, 80 per cent of the port managers of the country had held their position for five years or less. He states that "One of the obstacles to good port management and port development in the United States has been the rapid turnover of the managers."[24] The problem is a serious one in the development of good personnel and good administration.

Each of the two ports has an operations manager who is responsible to the executive director and is charged with the operation and maintenance of the port facilities.

The Authority also has three field representatives, one in New York City and two in North Carolina. Their general function is to acquaint business and industry with the advantages of using North Carolina seaports. The specific function of the New York representative is to maintain contact with shipping lines and with the headquarters offices of large shippers and receivers of ocean freight. The North Carolina representatives travel throughout the trade territory both as missionary salesmen and as solicitors of business for the two ports. The Authority has considered the advisability of having a representative in Chicago, but so far nothing has been done about the matter. Freight rates are competitive with those to other ports, but at present the Authority does not try to attract that business because the ports are unable to handle the extra tonnage.

At first the State Ports Authority had only an organization whose membership faced problems with which it was not familiar. There was no physical plant and building one required funds or capital. The Authority lacked funds, and no way had been provided for obtaining them except by the issuance of a small amount of revenue bonds. Without a plant and without traffic, it was not possible to sell this type of bond. The methods by which the Authority obtained funds to construct the original plant and then to expand it as traffic grew provide the subject matter of the following chapter.

[24] *Op. cit.*, p. 160.

2. Financing the State Ports

The act of 1945 which created the Authority did not provide for funds for administrative or promotional work, nor did the General Assembly appropriate any funds for the Authority at first. To start its program, under Title V of the War Mobilization and Reconversion Act of 1944, which authorized the Federal Works Agency to advance funds to non-federal public agencies to assist in the preparation of plans for worthy postwar projects, the Authority applied to the Bureau of Community Facilities of the Federal Works Agency for an advance of $90,000. That agency granted an amount of $88,738.37 for making a preliminary survey of the state's potential tonnage, the economic outlook for its ports, and cost estimates for the development of the different ports. A contract was made with a New York firm, at a cost of $25,000, to make a comprehensive industrial survey, particularly with the idea of developing state terminals at Wilmington and Morehead City. A contract also was made with an engineering firm in Atlanta, at a cost of $60,000, to prepare preliminary plans and specifications for a state terminal at Wilmington. Legal counsel was also employed by the Authority at a cost of $2,500. The Authority returned $1,238.37 of the grant to the Federal Works Agency.[1] The remainder of the grant was repaid in May, 1951. The preceding expenditures were approved and authorized by the General Assembly.[2]

The Authority is empowered to apply for and accept loans and grants of funds from any federal agency or the State of North Carolina or any of its subdivisions for any of the purposes authorized in the act and to spend the money in accordance with directions and requirements attached or imposed. None of such indebtedness, however, shall constitute an indebtedness of the state or any of its political subdivisions nor involve the credit or taxing power of the state or any of its political subdivisions.

[1] H. V. Conly, Assistant Director, North Carolina State Ports Authority, "North Carolina State Ports Authority: Its Origin, Construction and Development," June 26, 1953, p. 2. Mimeographed.
[2] H.B. 188, 1951 Session.

In June, 1946, the Authority asked the Council of State for $25,000 annually for administrative purposes beginning with the fiscal year July 1, 1946. Before this date it had been operating on the grant mentioned previously. The act establishing the Authority authorized the governor and the Council of State to allocate to the Authority such amounts from the Contingency and Emergency Fund as might from time to time actually be necessary for its maintenance and operation in carrying out the purposes of the act, but in no case were such funds to be in excess of $25,000 annually.[3] An appropriation of $50,000 annually for the biennium 1947-1949 was made available for the purpose of conducting investigations and preparing preliminary plans. These activities included (1) acquiring a suitable site, (2) making a state-wide survey to find out what facilities were needed or desired by shippers of the state, and (3) drawing up plans and specifications for the construction of at least one state port comparable to any other port on the South Atlantic coast as soon as a definite and suitable site was available.[4]

One of the first acts of the Authority was the start of negotiations with the United States Maritime Commission for a lease on the northern extension of the federal shipyard at Wilmington as the site for the state terminal. In November, 1949, after about three years of negotiation, the Maritime Commission signed a fifty-year lease under a dollar-a-year contract. In addition to this tract, consisting of approximately eighty acres, about twenty-nine adjoining acres were purchased, at $1,000 an acre, in order to provide for future expansion.

Under this agreement the federal government reserved the right in the event of a national emergency to terminate the lease or to declare it suspended or inoperative for the whole or any part of the property, with the payment of compensation or of a reasonable rental, as the case might be. In the opinion of competent authorities, these features were obstacles to the use of revenue bonds in financing port development. In the event that the federal government did have to exercise its rights, the conditions regarding compensation did not protect the owners of revenue bonds against default. In recognition of this problem, the Authority in 1956 acquired 323 acres of land on the west bank of the Brunswick River in Brunswick County which it

[3] "Port Authority Seeks $25,000 Grant Annually," *Durham Morning Herald,* June 6, 1946, 1:3.
[4] *Ibid.*

offered to the Maritime Commission in exchange for the government property now occupied and that adjacent to it.

In July, 1961, at a meeting after it had been sworn in, the board appointed by Governor H. Terry Sanford agreed to lease 115 additional acres adjacent to State Docks from the Maritime Commission. In November, 1961, the Navy Department decided that the Wilmington shipyard was no longer necessary for mobilization purposes, and North Carolina agreed to lease the remainder of the property for ten years at a rental of one dollar a year plus maintenance. The state further agreed to buy the shipyard for $445,000 plus the cost of buildings after the lease expires.[5] It may be noted here that there is plenty of available land for expanding State Docks, but Ocean Terminals at Morehead City has run out of land (see n. 13).

Appropriations for the Authority by fiscal years are shown in Table 2, along with the amounts requested by the Authority, the amounts recommended by the Bureau of the Budget, and the portions of the appropriations actually spent. Since they were opened for business about mid-1952, the state terminals have received revenue from operations that now amounts to much more than the state appropriations annually.

The Authority thus receives funds from two different sources, namely, state appropriations and port operations, and the spending of the funds from each source must be accounted for separately. There are, therefore, two broad classes of expenses. First are those expenses arising out of the functioning of the Authority itself, and second are those resulting from the operations of the ports. The former class of expenses is met by state appropriations, and the latter by income from operations insofar as it is adequate for the purpose. Deficits would have to be met by state appropriations, with the exception of interest on revenue bonds.

Under the law, the Budget Bureau has complete control over the expenditure of state-appropriated funds. The Authority has complete control over operating funds, without reference to any other state office, except that any net earnings must be paid to the state treasurer after the necessary reserves for operating capital and for making additions and improvements have been set aside, subject to the approval of the governor and the Council of State. The sums paid to the state treasurer are credited to a fund called the State Ports

[5] *Durham Morning Herald,* Nov. 9, 1961, B:3.

Bond Sinking Fund and thus become additional security for bonds which are obligations of the state.

The Buckley Report criticizes this use of the net earnings and suggests that the Bond Act of 1949, which is discussed later in this chapter, be modified to permit the Authority to retain these earnings in a reserve to be used for the payment of the principal and interest on revenue bonds which might be issued. Such a feature would make revenue bonds more attractive to investors and thus strengthen the ability of the Authority to use them.[6]

The data of Table 2 show the differences in opinion between the Authority, the General Assembly, and the Bureau of the Budget in respect to the amount of funds which the Authority needed or should have had. Not all of the appropriation was spent each year. The unspent balances were returned to the state treasury.

Table 2. Funds Requested, Recommended, Appropriated, and Actually Spent, for the State Ports Authority for Fiscal Years Ending June 30

Year	Requested	Recommended	Appropriation	Actual Expenditure
1948	$ —	$ —	$ 50,000	$ 13,445
1949	50,000[a]	—	50,000	43,921
1950	220,814[b]	50,000	50,000	35,517
1951	220,814	50,000[c]	50,000	40,523
1952	170,664[d]	48,860	74,460	51,405
1953	171,960	48,860	110,060	99,800
1954	177,512	80,308	126,652	107,538
1955	178,448	81,708	128,052	114,686
1956	287,392	194,733	192,633	154,152
1957	291,268	196,257	194,157	167,017
1958	262,867	174,046	174,076	171,236
1959	265,248	176,427	176,427	182,353
1960	273,187	182,778	182,778	177,491
1961	268,834	182,808	182,808	178,853
1962	199,527	199,527	199,527	—
1963	199,227	199,227	199,227	—

[a] Includes $12,500 for Reserve.
[b] Includes $135,914 for Reserve.
[c] Includes $12,050 for Reserve.
[d] Includes $27,740 for Reserve.
Source: Biennial Reports of the Advisory Budget Commission of North Carolina and Budget Reports of the State Ports Authority.

The Authority did not obtain funds for construction purposes until 1949, when a bond act was passed by the General Assembly. The act which created the Authority gave it the power to issue negotiable revenue bonds in an amount not to exceed $1,000,000. The

[6] P. 167.

State Ports Bond Act of 1949 authorized the issue of $7,500,000 of bonds of the state to provide for the construction of seaports.[7]

On November 3, 1948, the Authority had requested an appropriation of $7,558,372 from the state's general surplus to develop port facilities. Of the sum requested, the plans called for the use of $5,869,385 at Wilmington and $1,688,987 at Morehead City. The executive director had stressed to the Advisory Budget Commission that facilities were compulsory at both ports if a greater volume of shipping was to be developed.

Governor Scott, after assuming office, stated that the Authority was "withering" as then constituted.[8] Soon after, the entire board resigned, each member stating a desire to see the ports developed and a willingness to serve if reappointed. Only three of the seven members were reappointed, and one of those, A. G. Myers, vice-chairman of the previous board, became chairman.

Governor Scott spearheaded the movement for port improvements and was instrumental in obtaining the original appropriation for construction.[9] Under his administration the ports legislation was changed to make the director of the State Department of Conservation and Development a member ex officio of the Authority. With Governor Scott's encouragement, the Department of Conservation and Development established a special committee to work with the Authority to help it realize its goals and obtain an appropriation for construction purposes.

At first the Authority encountered difficulty in obtaining support for the development of seaports except at the seaports themselves. In regard to this problem, Charles M. Johnson, state treasurer, stated that, "It is unfortunate that people in North Carolina have come to regard port development as a special interest of Wilmington and Morehead City, while as a matter of fact both ports are of benefit to the entire state. If the latter were not true, port development would be worth nothing to Wilmington."[10]

Executive Director Col. George W. Gillette, in commenting on the lack of interest in Piedmont and western North Carolina, also pointed out that port development would not be for the sole benefit of the port cities. In a speech to the Rotary Club of Gastonia, North

[7] Session Laws of North Carolina 1949, chap. 820.
[8] *Durham Morning Herald*, Jan. 27, 1949, 12:1.
[9] *New York Times*, Aug. 12, 1952, 43:4.
[10] *Durham Morning Herald*, Aug. 22, 1947, 2:7.

Carolina, on December 30, 1948, he said: "It would save North Carolina manufacturers millions of dollars annually in freights on imported raw materials and would at the same time enable industries of this state to compete much more effectively with similar industries in other areas."[11]   As an example he said that at the time all of the mahogany wood used in North Carolina furniture factories came from South America through Boston, with freight cost that was $27 per unit higher than if brought through North Carolina ports.

The Bond Act of 1949 provided for the issue of State Port Bonds for sale at one time or from time to time.   The bonds were to be serial bonds ending not later than twenty years after issue, and the rate of interest was not to be more than 4 per cent.   The faith and credit of the state were pledged for the payment of both principal and interest. The bonds were not to be subject to state, county, or municipal taxes or assessments and they were to be legal investments for fiduciary funds.

On August 9, 1949, the state sold $7,500,000 of six-month Ports Bond Anticipation Notes to the First Securities Corporation of Durham, N. C., at a discount of 0.5223 per cent.   On November 15, 1950, the state issued $7,500,000 of State Ports Bonds, the proceeds being used to retire the Ports Bond Anticipation Notes.[12]   The interest rate, varying with the maturity date, averaged 1.412711 per cent.

The Authority decided to spend $5 million of this amount at Wilmington and $2.5 million at Morehead City.   The resulting construction program was completed in 1952.   The state port at Morehead City was dedicated on August 14, 1952, and that at Wilmington on September 16, following.[13]   The construction program for these ports was only in its beginning, however, as will become evident shortly.   But the construction that was completed at this time did place the state ports in a position to start bidding for traffic.   The Authority

[11] *Ibid.*, Dec. 31, 1948, 1:2.

[12] The proceeds from the sale of the State Ports Bonds were put in the State Ports Authority Fund, from which they were appropriated to the State Ports Authority to be used "for construction, reconstruction, enlargement or improvement of seaports in N.C., including but not confined to the acquisition, construction, reconstruction, enlargement, improvement of wharves, docks, warehouses, loading and unloading machinery and equipment, and other terminal buildings, structures, and facilities useful and proper in the operation of seaports" (Session Laws of North Carolina 1949, chap. 820).

[13] The official name of the state terminal at Morehead City is North Carolina Ocean Terminals and at Wilmington it is North Carolina State Docks.   Hereinafter, the names Ocean Terminals and State Docks will be used for the state facilities at Morehead City and Wilmington, respectively.

had proceeded with the idea of future expansion expressly incorporated in its plans. The General Assembly, however, always has been slow in meeting the requests of the Authority for funds for expansion.

The reader will note that the issue of $7.5 million in state bonds was authorized under the Bond Act of 1949, whereas the act of 1945 authorized the issue by the Authority of revenue bonds not to exceed $1 million in amount. Obviously, without any facilities for accomodating traffic before terminals were constructed, the Authority was in no position to issue revenue bonds that were to be supported from the earnings of the venture. There also was a legal problem.

The Attorney General of North Carolina was not certain that the Authority had the legal power to issue negotiable revenue bonds and believed that the net revenues of the Authority would be held and pledged for the payment of the $7.5 million issue of State Ports Bonds. Because of this uncertainty in respect to obtaining funds, the Authority was compelled to forego certain contracts for traffic which it believed would have been profitable.[14] The question was not settled definitely until July 1, 1955, when, in a test case brought by the state, the Supreme Court of North Carolina approved the financing of port facilities by the use of revenue bonds. The Authority had plans for issuing $60,000 of such bonds for financing the construction of a grain elevator at Morehead City. The elevator already had been built at a cost of $80,000. The remaining $20,000 was to be obtained from port earnings. These bonds were issued and the final instalment on the principal was paid off on January 1, 1960. The elevator had been leased for five years to Cargill, Inc. The Authority also had hopes of financing a multi-million dollar truck terminal in a similar manner. If constructed, this terminal was to be leased to the McLean Trucking Company for truck-boat operations.[15] On March 3, 1954, the Authority had agreed to issue $2,500,000 in revenue bonds to construct such a terminal if the McLean plan for hauling loaded trailers by boat was approved by the Interstate Commerce Commission. This project never materialized.

One should be aware that these two cities were not without port facilities before the state ports were constructed, but they did not have channels deep enough or shore facilities proper for handling appreciable amounts of general cargo. Both places had had some

[14] Conly, op. cit., pp. 8-9.
[15] Raleigh News and Observer, July 1, 1955, 1:6.

traffic for a century or more, and Wilmington had attracted a considerable amount of commerce when the production of naval stores and the growing of cotton had been important in its hinterland. The decline in these two industries and the rise of cotton manufacturing in the Piedmont, reducing cotton exports still more, were factors in the later demands for aid for the port.

In addition to the proceeds of the original bond issue, the Authority has received state appropriations for capital investments and has used a portion of its own net earnings for the same purpose. The sum of the par value of the bond issue and the state appropriations for enlarging and improving the ports is carried in the balance sheet of the Authority as "surplus donated by the State" (see Table 3).

In 1957 the General Assembly appropriated $3,390,000 and in 1959 allocated $917,000 for expanding port facilities. Of the former amount, approximately $2,600,000 was allocated to Wilmington and almost $800,000 to Morehead City. Wilmington received $560,000 and Morehead City $357,000 of the 1959 appropriation. These appropriations were in addition to those made annually for general administration and maintenance. For the period 1947-1959, the General Assembly appropriated a total of $12,307,400 for capital improvements at the two ports.[16] The additions to the plant made with the 1957 appropriation were put into use during 1960. During the period 1955-1960 the Authority plowed back almost $1.25 million from its earnings into capital improvements.[17]

The 1961 General Assembly made provision for a state-wide referendum on an issue of $13,500,000 of 20-year, 3.5 per cent bonds for improving and expanding the two state terminals. The issuance of these bonds was defeated by the voters of the state in November, 1961. The facilities that were to be provided with the funds from the sale of these bonds are described in a later chapter.

To date, the Authority has not been able to repay much on the bonded indebtedness which is carried by the state and for which the Authority is contingently liable. On June 30, 1960, there was $3,220,000 in outstanding bonds and $227,927 had been paid into the "State Ports Bond Sinking Fund."[18] A comparison of the annual

[16] *The Budget 1961-63,* II, 83.
[17] See statement of Executive Director D. Leon Williams in *North Carolina State Ports,* Summer, 1960, p. 5.
[18] See the Biennial Report of the Treasurer of North Carolina, 1959-60, pp. 89, 92.

appropriations by the state for the Authority (see Table 2) with the net profit after depreciation from operations (see Table 30) will reveal that these appropriations amount to more than the net earnings. No provision has been made for amortizing the investment which the state has made in determining the net profit.

Opinions differ in regard to the extent to which a port authority should be compelled to meet the total economic cost of the enterprise. Some people believe a port should be self-supporting; others hold that only enough revenue to cover marginal costs, largely operating expenses, should be expected.[19] The legislation of the different states with port authorities does not require the activities to be financially self-sufficient, but the implication is clear that revenues from operations are expected to pay operating and maintenance costs plus interest on bonded indebtedness. However, to develop, a state-sponsored revenue-collecting enterprise must have the assurance of financial support by the state, and if the state must absorb deficits, an over-all loss to the state is not indicated. There may be gains to the economy of the state.[20] In the United States a seaport is generally recognized as a public utility. "General harbor works and terminal facilities are rightly an object of public finance, as they serve the people directly or indirectly for a period of many years and therefore come under the category of public utilities as waterworks, parks, and subways, etc."[21] On this matter the Buckley Report expresses the opinion that the general interests of the state apparently justify a continuing appropriation from general revenues to administer the state port facilities and to protect and promote its water-borne commerce.

The Authority paid $201,800 for the facilities at Morehead City, this sum being the amount still owed by the the Port Commission on $326,000 in bonds purchased by the Reconstruction Finance Corporation in a transaction mentioned previously. These bonds were secured by the earnings of the Atlantic and North Carolina Railroad Company, and they had been assumed by the Authority under the terms of a seventy-five-year lease of November 15, 1949, under which the facilities of the Port Commission were leased by the Authority. On April 1, 1951, the Port Commission transferred its

[19] See Fair, *op. cit.*, p. 143.

[20] See E. Schenker, "Southern State Port Authorities and Florida," *Land Economics*, XXXV, 40-41 (1958).

[21] R. S. MacElwee, *Port Development* (New York, 1926), p. 52.

functions and the title to its properties to the Authority. The agreement provided that the Port Commission would operate the facilities until the Authority was ready to take control, after which time the Port Commission was to pass out of existence.[22]

[22] Session Laws of North Carolina 1951, chap. 776.

Table 3. Balance Sheet of the North Carolina State Ports Authority June 30, 1961

ASSETS			
Current Assets			
Cash		$	$ 284,341
Accounts Receivable			
Trade		59,229	
Other		547	59,776
Investments			437,393
Total Current Assets			781,510
Properties			
Plant & Equipment—Wilmington		8,202,220	
Plant & Equipment—Morehead City		4,435,393	
Administrative Assets		18,820	
Total Depreciable Properties		12,656,433	
Less: Reserve for Depreciation		1,763,595	
Total Depreciable Properties—Net		10,892,838	
Chemical Storage Facilities—Dow		25,155	
Construction in Progress		52,950	
Land		216,958	
Total Properties—Net			11,187,901
Other Assets			
Unalloted Appropriations		231,831	
Unexpended Allotments		38,351	
Inventory of Materials		8,540	
Prepaid Insurance & Sundry		14,483	
Total Other Assets			293,205
Total Assets			12,262,616
LIABILITIES AND SURPLUS			
Current Liabilities			
Accounts Payable			1,164
Payroll Deductions & Accruals			10,194
Total Current Liabilities			11,358
Deferred Credit to Income			
Income Received—Not Earned			938
Long-Term Indebtedness			
Notes Payable			70,883
Surplus			
Donated by State—Capital Improvements		11,697,400	
Earned—Exhibit "B"		482,037	12,179,437
Total Liabilities & Surplus			12,262,616

Source: State Ports Authority, Exhibit "A."

The facilities obtained from the Morehead City Port Commission consisted of two docks, a transit shed, railroad tracks, loading and unloading equipment, a water tank, an office, and general port paraphernalia and equipment. The acquisition of these facilities is the reason for the allocation of more funds from the original bond issue to Wilmington than to Morehead City for construction purposes. The policy of the Authority in this matter has been to provide each port with approximately equal facilities.

Assets, Liabilities, and Surplus

Table 3 is the balance sheet of the State Ports Authority for the fiscal year 1960-1961. As one would expect, the assets consist largely of fixed plant and equipment. The investment at Wilmington is almost double that at Morehead City. The liabilities consist almost entirely of the investment by the state in the ports.

The following chapter describes the existing physical plant, including the harbors and channels which have been improved and maintained largely by the federal government. The harbors are not used exclusively by the state terminals, and improvements had been made on them long before the state terminals were built.

3. The North Carolina Seaports: Characteristics, Facilities, and Services

A seaport consists of a harbor; of the fixed plant and equipment required for moving, loading, and unloading products, including storage facilities; of physical connections with railroads and highways; and of various facilitating services such as a shipper's agent, freight handlers, freight forwarders, vessel agents, vessel service agencies, financial institutions, insurance agents, and numerous federal and state agencies.

The Harbor at Morehead City

The port at Morehead City is on Bogue Sound, a shallow body of water about two miles in width near its middle portion and narrower toward each end, extending from Beaufort Inlet twenty-two miles westward to Bogue Inlet.[1] Bogue Banks separates Bogue Sound from the Atlantic Ocean. Entrance from the Atlantic Ocean is by way of Beaufort Inlet, situated between Bogue Banks and Shackleford Banks four miles from Morehead City.

The tides have a mean range of 2.5 feet at Morehead City, and in Bogue Sound they vary from an average of 2.5 feet near the middle to about one foot at intermediate points. Strong south or southwest winds may raise the tides a foot or more, and north and northwest

[1] "The Port" (originally "The Point"), a nose of land jutting out between Bogue Sound and the mouth of the Newport River, was a natural landing place in the early nineteenth century. John Motley Morehead, a governor of the state, saw its potential as a seaport and bought the point which, with surrounding acreage, eventually became Morehead City. A pier and small warehouse with rail facilities were built. Lime and salt were brought in and naval stores were loaded for northern ports, and the rails for the railroad to Goldsboro were imported from England.

The Civil War brought shipping to a halt and in 1879 a storm did considerable damage. Commercial shipping began again in 1880 by small craft. Large vessels sought more modern ports. The wharf went into disrepair after the railroad was extended to Beaufort. During World War I the port was converted into a small shipyard for building government ships. In 1945 the port property was leased to the Standard Oil Company, and in 1951 it was sold to the State Ports Authority. (For an account of the history of the port at Morehead City, see an article by Ruth Peeling, editor of the *Carteret County News-Times*, in *North Carolina State Ports*, Fall, 1960, p. 13.)

winds have a reverse effect. At the entrance the tidal currents have a velocity of two to three knots an hour, and they usually run parallel with the channel.

Pilotage is compulsory from the ocean to the terminal for vessels in foreign trade and those in coastwise service except those under sixty tons or steam vessels with a pilot licensed by the United States Steamboat Inspection Service on board. Ships proceed from the ocean to the terminal and back without the assistance of a tug. Anchorages are not available at Morehead City Harbor.

Morehead City became a factor in deep-water commerce in 1936 when the federal government completed a thirty-foot channel and the municipality completed construction of public port facilities. Previously, fishing fleets and shallow draft commercial boats had operated from the port. In spite of the improved harbor and terminal, the volume of traffic and general cargo in particular remained low. Growth was almost entirely in petroleum products. In 1957 Congress gave top priority for the further improvement of Beaufort Inlet Channel and Morehead City Harbor, and in the spring of 1960 Army engineers began work on the project. This improvement calls for a 35-foot channel 400 feet wide increasing to 600 feet at the bend, thence a channel 35 feet deep and 300 feet wide and an enlarged turning basin 35 feet deep, then a 12-foot channel 100 feet wide to Sixth Street and a 35-foot channel 200 feet to 400 feet wide to Tenth Street, and finally a 6-foot channel 75 feet wide to deep water in Bogue Sound.[2] (See Figure 1.)

The federal government recently installed a new range system on Pivers Island which makes the harbor more attractive to deep-water navigation. This system is an important aid in navigating Beaufort Inlet and provides twenty-four-hour service at Ocean Terminals.[3]

As is commonly known, the federal government has the responsibility for improving and maintaining the harbors of the nation. The total amount spent to June 30, 1960, on the harbor at Morehead City was $4,344,465, of which one-fifth roughly was for new work and four-fifths was for maintenance.[4]

[2] *Annual Report,* Chief of Engineers, U. S. Army, 1960, Civil Works Activities, II, 351.
[3] L. C. Bruce, Director of Public Relations, State Ports Authority, "Tonnage, Revenue Records Set During '60 by N. C. Ports," *Durham Morning Herald,* Dec. 25, 1960, C:11.
[4] *Annual Report,* Chief of Engineers, U. S. Army, 1960, II, 353-354.

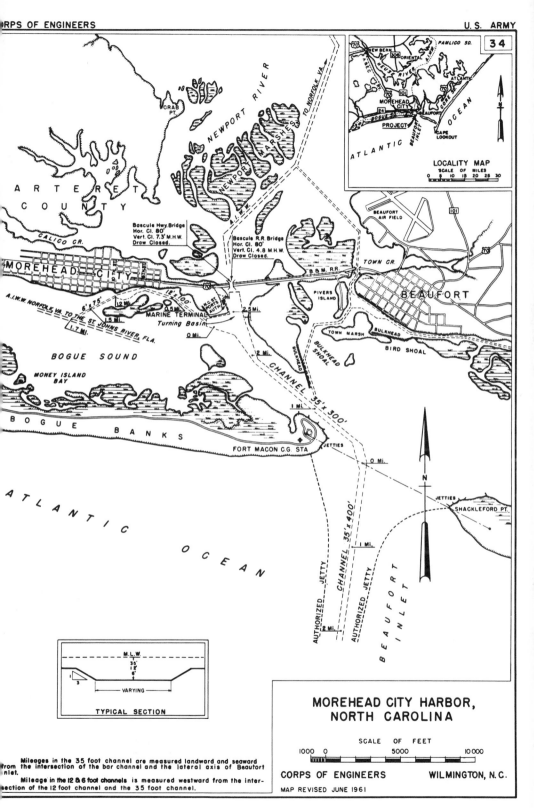

Figure 1.

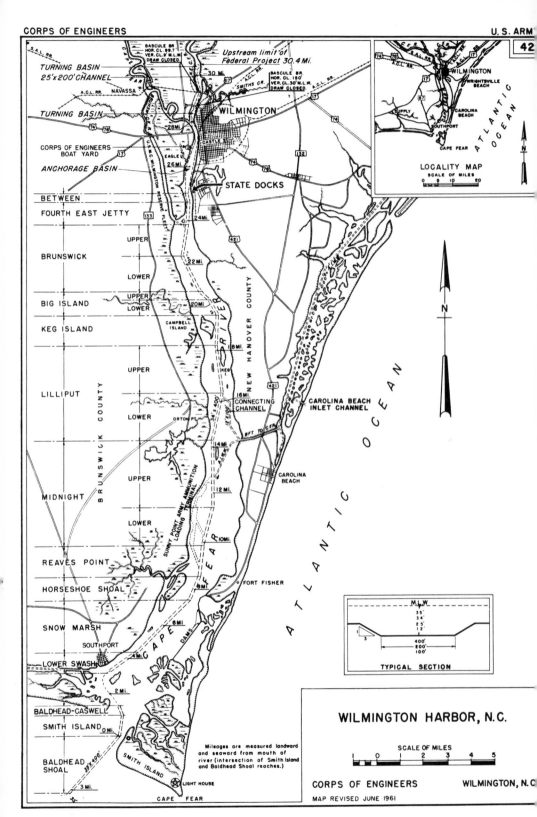

42

Upstream limit of Federal Project 30.4 Mi.

TURNING BASIN 25' x 200' CHANNEL
TURNING BASIN
NAVASSA
A.C.L. RR.
WILMINGTON
CORPS OF ENGINEERS BOAT YARD
ANCHORAGE BASIN
STATE DOCKS
BETWEEN
FOURTH EAST JETTY
BRUNSWICK
UPPER
LOWER
BIG ISLAND
UPPER
LOWER
KEG ISLAND
CAMPBELL ISLAND
LILLIPUT
UPPER
LOWER
ORTON PT.
MIDNIGHT
UPPER
LOWER
REAVES POINT
HORSESHOE SHOAL
SNOW MARSH
SOUTHPORT
LOWER SWASH
BALDHEAD-CASWELL
SMITH ISLAND
BALDHEAD SHOAL

BRUNSWICK COUNTY

NEW HANOVER COUNTY

CONNECTING CHANNEL

CAROLINA BEACH INLET CHANNEL

CAROLINA BEACH

FORT FISHER

ATLANTIC OCEAN

CAPE FEAR RIVER

SUNNY POINT ARMY AMMUNITION LOADING TERMINAL

SMITH ISLAND
LIGHT HOUSE
CAPE FEAR

Mileages are measured landward and seaward from mouth of river (intersection of Smith Island and Baldhead Shoal reaches.)

LOCALITY MAP
SCALE OF MILES

WILMINGTON
WRIGHTSVILLE BEACH
CAROLINA BEACH
SOUTHPORT
CAPE FEAR
ATLANTIC OCEAN

N

TYPICAL SECTION
MLW
35'
34'
25'
12'
400'
200'
100'

WILMINGTON HARBOR, N.C.

SCALE OF MILES
1 0 1 2 3 4 5

CORPS OF ENGINEERS   WILMINGTON, N.C

MAP REVISED JUNE 1961

Figure 2.

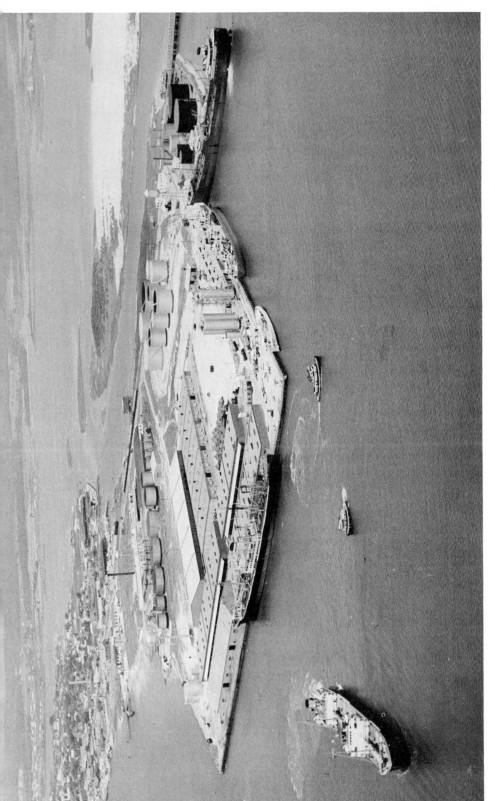

Figure 3. Ocean Terminals, Morehead City (courtesy N. C. State Ports Authority)

Figure 4. State Docks, Wilmington (courtesy N. C. State Ports Authority)

The Harbor at Wilmington

The port of Wilmington is located thirty miles inland from the Atlantic Ocean on the Cape Fear River. At Wilmington the Northeast (Cape Fear) River, the lower portion of which is included in the Wilmington port district, joins the Cape Fear; Smith's Creek joins the Northeast River at the northern edge of Wilmington. The Brunswick River, which is outside the limits of the port of Wilmington, branches from the Cape Fear River about three miles above the city, flows southeastward for five miles, and then rejoins that river about four miles below the city and across from and slightly below State Docks.

The mean range of tides at the mouth of the Cape Fear River is 4.7 feet and at Wilmington, 3.4 feet. Tidal currents at the mouth of the river are strong and usually run parallel with the channel. On the river tidal currents are usually parallel with the channel, and the velocity depends upon the stage of the river. During heavy rains the flood stage of the river predominates, but during low water the tidal currents predominate. At low water there is a strong flood tide for a considerable distance above Wilmington where it runs five and a quarter hours, compared with nearly seven hours for the ebb tide. Downstream from Wilmington the periods of the flood and ebb tides are more nearly equal.

Pilotage is compulsory from the ocean to Southport for vessels in foreign trade and those in domestic trade with the same exception as given previously for Morehead City. Ships usually proceed from the ocean to Wilmington and back without the assistance of a towboat. A protected area of 2,100,000 square feet with a depth ranging from four to six fathoms in the Cape Fear River near Southport provides good anchorage. Coastwise ships sometimes use these waters as a harbor of refuge in winter.

Congress approved a 34-foot channel for Wilmington in 1950, but did not provide funds for the work until 1956. This project has been completed.

The present project at Wilmington has a channel 35 feet deep where the Cape Fear River enters the Atlantic and 34 feet deep from that point to the upper end of the anchorage basin which is midway between State Docks and the private terminals (see Figure 2), and

400 feet wide for the entire distance. The anchorage basin is 2,000 feet long and 900 feet wide at the upper end and 1,100 feet at the lower end. It has an approach 1,500 feet long at the upper end and one of 4,500 feet at the lower end. From the anchorage basin to the Hilton Bridge on the Northeast (Cape Fear) River the channel is 30 feet deep and 300 feet wide, and from the bridge to a point 1.25 miles above it the channel is 25 feet deep and 200 feet wide. On the Northeast River just above its junction with the Cape Fear River there is a turning basin 1,000 feet long and 800 feet wide, and 1.25 miles above the bridge there is another turning basin 600 feet wide. The Intracoastal Waterway enters the Cape Fear River through a land cut and extends northwestward to the main ship channel along a channel 12 feet deep and 100 feet wide. At a point four miles from the mouth of the river just below Southport the Intracoastal Waterway leaves the main channel on its route to Georgetown, South Carolina. The depths are all at mean low water. Two bridges cross the Cape Fear River at Wilmington and two cross the Northeast River within the port area. All four bridges are of the bascule type. State Docks is below these bridges.[5]

The total sum spent on the harbor and channel by the federal government at Wilmington to June 30, 1960, was $20,018,788. This sum was about equally divided between new work and maintenance.[6]

The recent improvements offer special advantages to petroleum carriers, whose large ships will be able to navigate the channel at full load under mean low water. The added depth is a safety measure for ships.

A plan to have the Cape Fear River deepened to forty feet has been advanced recently, after local surveys indicated a natural trough in the river bed near Southport with a depth exceeding forty feet. It has been stressed that the natural trough is the southernmost natural deep-water harbor on the Atlantic coast, and the advantages of this feature, in view of the development of larger tankers and bulk-load freighters, has been emphasized.[7] Officials of the State Ports Authority say they have no particular interest in deepening the channel to this depth, because the vessels that haul general cargo are not of a draft to require such depth.[8]

[5] *Ibid.*, II, 358-359.
[6] *Ibid.*, II, 361.
[7] *North Carolina State Ports*, Fall, 1957, p. 10.
[8] "Draft is . . . the distance from water level to the lowest point of the vessel

Terminal Facilities and Services

Important influences in attracting traffic to a seaport are the quantity and kinds of terminal facilities and the ease and degree of efficiency with which these facilities can handle cargoes. For several years after World War II North Carolina ports lost export and coastwise shipping (except petroleum products) to Charleston and Norfolk, both of which had aggressive port managements and modern port facilities. Commerce was diverted from North Carolina ports even when rail rates were in their favor because of the lack of modern facilities and services to handle traffic.[9] In some instances North Carolina seaports did not have rates because the particular products never had moved through them. For example, in 1947 this was found to be true of textiles in a survey made by the Industrial and Traffic Manager of the City of Wilmington.

Wilmington had facilities that were adequate for the commodities which had previously been moving through the port, but they were in a rundown condition and were unclean.[10] The consensus was that the port was not adequate for handling other kinds of freight, particularly general cargo.

The following discussion describes the existing terminal facilities at both state ports and indicates the extent to which the problem of providing modern general cargo terminals has been met.

Ocean Terminals

In 1961 Ocean Terminals (see Figure 3) had a wharf 2,550 feet in length with a 34-foot apron which could accommodate four 500-foot

underwater and is measured when the vessel is completely stopped—either tied to a dock or at anchor. The draft under way—while the vessel is moving—is dependent on many factors, such as speed of the vessel and depth and width of the channel, and varies from channel to channel. Channel depth of at least three feet more than the draft of a vessel at dock is required where vessels must be operated at low speed. Channel depth of five feet more than the draft of a vessel at dock is required in channels where vessels can be operated at more efficient and economical speeds." (*Waterborne Commerce of the United States,* Corps of Engineers, U.S. Army, Washington, D.C., 1956, Part I, p. IV.)

[9] Unsigned typewritten article in the files of the State Ports Authority in the State Department of Archives and History.

[10] There are better facilities now, owing to a fire which destroyed five of the warehouses of the upper harbor on March 9, 1953. Almost immediately private interests constructed a new modern bulk terminal which is operated by three firms (*North Carolina Ports,* Feb.-March, 1954, pp. 13-14).

vessels and one pertroleum tanker simultaneously at a depth of 35 feet at mean low water. There were three transit sheds and four warehouses with a combined capacity of 132,000 sq. ft. and 273,000 sq. ft., respectively, and an open storage area. There was also a grain elevator which could load 250 tons of grain an hour and a fumigation plant with a capacity of 76 hogsheads of tobacco. This plant was completed in 1957 and was built because of demands for it by tobacco shippers in order that tobacco leaf could meet the inspection requirements of the countries to which it is exported. It can be used for other products as well as tobacco. Other facilities included railway tracks and truck docks and equipment for the full palletization of general cargoes. The Southern Railway had a freight car storage yard adjacent to the terminal.[11]

In 1961 State Docks (see Figure 4) had a wharf 2,510 feet in length with a 46-foot apron which could accommodate five 500-foot vessels simultaneously at a depth of 34 feet at mean low water. There are three transit sheds and two storage warehouses with a total capacity of 266,000 sq. ft. and 186,000 sq. ft., respectively, and ten acres of paved open storage space. In addition there is a shed of 150,000 sq. ft. divided into five bays, each serviced by two overhead cranes, and a modern fumigation plant. This plant was built in 1954 and is one of the largest of its kind in the South. It was provided primarily for imported cotton, but it can be used for other products. A car storage yard has a capacity of 240 freight cars. Other facilities include railway tracks and truck docks, a weighing station, two 45-ton gantry cranes for heavy lifting, two smaller cranes, and equipment for the full palletization of general cargo.[12]

Before the construction of the state terminal the cargo handled at the port of Wilmington for the most part did not require heavy lifting equipment, although this condition may have prevailed because shippers knew the port did not have such equipment. In case a cargo

[11] *North Carolina State Ports,* June, 1961, p. 9.

In 1957 the port at Morehead City had 24 piers, 20 of which were for mooring or servicing small craft engaged in the fishing trade. None of the 20 piers was on the 30-foot channel and none had in excess of 200 feet in berthing space. Four piers were on the 30-foot channel and they were also directly on the Intracoastal Waterway. One of the four was a bulk liquid terminal and three were berths at the Authority terminal that were used for both liquid and general cargo (Buckley Report, p. 24).

[12] *North Carolina State Ports,* June, 1961, p. 8.

In 1957 Wilmington had 53 piers. Of this number 32 were unsuited to ocean-going vessels and of the remaining 21 only three had any capacity for general cargo. Of these three only State Docks had modern construction and layout. The only modern private facilities were those used for bulk cargoes (Buckley Report, p. 27).

requiring heavy lifting equipment was accepted, the equipment might be hired, although the amount available for hire was limited. Inasmuch as the Authority is trying to attract general cargo to its terminals, the necessity for the required modern equipment is evident. Such equipment provides for more flexible operations and more rapid handling and makes possible the handling of a variety of commodities.[13]

The Authority has improved and expanded the plant, equipment, and services of the state terminals as their commerce has grown. Modern buildings and modern cargo-handling equipment and facilties have been provided, with additions as new demands arise within the limits of the available funds. The trend at Ocean Terminals is toward specialized facilities for the handling of liquid and dry bulk cargoes, such as petroleum, tobacco, and grain. At State Docks the trend is toward facilities adapted to a greater volume of general cargo. This development came about because Wilmington has better rail and truck services than Morehead City and because Wilmington has an advantage over Morehead City in freight rates on many articles.

A comparison of the preceding facilities with those at the time the state ports were first opened for business in 1952 shows how much the facilities and the investment in the ports have grown. When operations began, the plant and equipment were those provided by the $7.5 million bond issue of 1950 plus those that had been purchased from the Morehead City Port Commission (see p. 26).

In 1952 Ocean Terminals had a wharf 2,550 feet long which would berth four 500-foot cargo ships and one petroleum tanker simultaneously. Two transit sheds had a combined capacity of 92,000 sq. ft. and two storage warehouses a total capacity of 176,000 sq. ft. A paved open storage area contained 60,000 sq. ft. There was equipment for the full palletization of cargoes.

State Docks had a wharf 1,510 feet long that would accommodate three 500-foot ships. Two transit sheds had a combined capacity of 158,000 sq. ft., and one storage warehouse had a capacity of 86,100 sq. ft. A paved open storage area contained three acres. There was equipment for the full palletization of cargoes and one 40-ton and one 25-ton locomotive crane.

The Buckley Report estimated that in 1957 Morehead City had a total annual capacity of 2,300,000 tons for handling traffic and

[13] *North Carolina State Ports*, June, 1957, p. 12.

Wilmington a capacity of 7,200,000 tons. Both figures were well above the then current volume of traffic and the volume anticipated by some, and since then the capacity at both ports has been increased. The preceding statements, it should be noted, apply to the entire port at each city, and not just to the state terminals. At Morehead City, Ocean Terminals does account for almost the entire tonnage, but at Wilmington private facilities, some open to the public and some exclusively for the product of their owners, handle much more tonnage annually than does State Docks.

However, the capacity at Morehead City for general cargo, as distinguished from bulk items, was 182,000 tons, a figure still above present or prospective general cargo tonnage. At Wilmington three general cargo piers had a combined capacity of 272,500 tons, which was well above actual utilization. Most of the general cargo, however, must use State Docks which had about reached capacity. At both state terminals the provision of sufficient space for storing leaf tobacco was a problem.[14]

Currently, facilities are heavily taxed at both state ports. Frequent congestion, particularly at State Docks, indicates a need for more berths and more storage space. At State Docks ships are often delayed by having to wait at anchor, some are diverted to private docks, and sometimes business is refused because of inability to handle the ship and the cargo. In addition, transit sheds are often overflowing and freight cars are sometimes held in demurrage at the expense of the Authority because space is unavailable in the transit sheds. Because of these conditions, makeshift methods must be employed, and some cargoes must be handled several times in the transit sheds or in the yards, all of which increases operating costs. The Operations Manager at Ocean Terminals stated that "at least 30 per cent of our net profits are being lost because of this extra handling of cargo."[15]

At present, a need exists for storage capacity permitting storage for extended periods awaiting shipment or sale. Such facilities permit an exporter to accumulate a cargo gradually and thus save storage and an additional handling charge at an inland point. The accumulated storage attracts ships because of the larger cargoes available.

[14] Buckley Report, pp. 105, 111-112.
[15] See C. S. Davis, "Too Little, But It's Not Too Late," Winston-Salem *Journal and Sentinel,* July 31, 1960, D:1.

A relationship exists between the storage capacity at a port and the number and frequency of sailing schedules. Importers like to sell and distribute from the port of entry; adequate storage capacity there makes it possible for them to maintain an inventory for the purpose.

At the state ports exporters are allowed seventeen days in which to accumulate a cargo in the transit shed and ship it out. Importers have five days for moving their cargo from the ship, through the transit shed, and out of the port. If longer periods than these are required, a place is needed where the cargoes can be stored.

Ordinary cargoes can be moved into a dock warehouse for long-term storage when the limits are overstayed in the transit shed, but at both state ports the warehouses are packed to capacity, particularly at Ocean Terminals because of the importance of tobacco as an export. At present, this port has storage capacity for 30,000 hogsheads of tobacco. More storage space is needed for tobacco leaf than for the normal handling of average general cargoes. Tobacco is produced seasonally, large amounts may be forwarded to a port even before a sale is made or shipping instructions are known, and because it must be aged, it may be stored for periods of a few weeks to as long as three years or more.

The management consulting firm of Cresap, McCormick, and Paget, which made the exhaustive study used by the Authority as the basis for its request to the General Assembly of 1961 for $13.5 million for improvements and expansion, stated that the state will be injured industrially and neighboring states will be directly aided if this program is not launched.[16] This firm recommended an expenditure of $8 million at State Docks and one of $5.5 million at Ocean Terminals. These amounts would provide, respectively, three new berths and two new transit sheds at State Docks and one new berth, one new transit shed, and a grain elevator at Ocean Teminals. The grain elevator would cost $1.25 million.[17]

Basing its conclusions on the revenue to be received from the projected increase of 118 per cent in tonnage, the consulting firm stated the Authority could pay off 97 per cent of the principal and interest of the bond issue from operations. It was pointed out that

[16] See statements by E. F. Bofferding, a partner of the firm, in "Speaker Cites Need to Expand N. C. Ports," *Durham Morning Herald*, July 23, 1961, A:2.
[17] In 1957 the State of South Carolina authorized an investment of $21 million in port development, and at the same time a bond issue of $40 million was proposed for the same purpose in Virginia.

a building program involving $21 million at Charleston had brought about the predicted increase in traffic there. New industries located in the Charleston area because of the modern port facilities and the frequent sailings from the port.

Of course, all ports or potential ports cannot hope to invest in expansions indefinitely and expect to pay for the expansion with new revenue. In their competition with each other, a point would ultimately be reached where ports would only maintain their relative positions at a gradually growing cost.

Both of the state terminals provide water, telephone, and electrical service, a security force on duty at all times, and a federally approved supply of drinking water at shipside. Oil terminals at each port provide a bunkering service for ships,[18] but there are no coal bunkering services. Neither terminal has cold storage facilities, but the provision of such service is now being considered.

In addition to having the physical facilities for handling cargoes, a seaport also must offer the necessary services for receiving and dispatching shipments. Such services include forwarding, contracting for space on the boat, stevedoring for loading and unloading, and filling out the necessary documents. At the state terminal at Wilmington there is limited space available for firms providing shipping services, and in September, 1953, the Authority agreed to allow shipping agents, forwarders, and others to lease space. One shipping firm applied for space, but when the two others opposed the application, the Authority agreed to offer space to all three within the limits of the available space.[19]

The Morehead Shipping Company, a branch of the Wilmington Shipping Company, the first to apply for space at Wilmington, was organized early in 1954 and was the first major shipping agency to locate permanent offices at Morehead City. It is a complete shipping agency, providing forwarding and stevedoring services. Morehead City previously had been served by the parent company of Wilmington, this company being the representative of a number of steamship companies, exporters, and importers.

Heide and Company, Inc., is another Wilmington firm which provides the same kinds of services as the Wilmington Shipping Com-

---

[18] Each issue of *North Carolina State Ports* has a list of all the different facilities at each state terminal.
[19] *Durham Morning Herald,* Sept. 15, 1953, 1:2.

pany. The parent firm, the Hiede Warehouse Company, furnishes storage services, handling nothing but bulk cargoes. Heide and Company, Inc., moves all but bulk cargoes through other terminals than its own, including the State Docks.

The Waters Shipping Company is a recently organized one with offices at State Docks in Wilmington. The firm will specialize in international freight forwarding and custom house brokerage.

Another recently introduced service in a different field is the financing of foreign trade by the International Department of the Wachovia Bank and Trust Company, which was established in its Wilmington branch during 1960. This move was made to stimulate trade by Carolina firms with the markets of the world by providing services formerly not directly available in the Carolinas. The importance of this specialized service may be illustrated by the example of an exporter of textiles in Charlotte who maintained an additional office in Atlanta because of the Foreign Department of the Atlanta bank; his exports naturally moved through Savannah.[20] Wachovia also serves as an agent of the Export-Import Bank of Washington, D. C., for export credit insurance covering certain short-term political risks.

A proposal in the early plans for facilities at Wilmington was the obtaining of a floating Navy drydock. Wilmington has the double disadvantage of being situated far to the west of the main coastwise route and inland thirty miles on the Cape Fear River. Ship operators hesitate to go so far from their principal paths unless they are assured of enough traffic regularly to make the trip profitable. The Authority believed that the drydock would be an inducement for ships to call for repair and maintenance service, and that, in so doing, they would bring imports with them and also be in a position to carry away exports.

Negotiations for obtaining the drydock were unsuccessful, how-

[20] "The Ports Problem," *The State,* May 2, 1953, p. 5.
The services a bank's foreign department can offer importers include (1) opening letters of credit to finance imports, (2) selling foreign exchange necessary to pay for imports purchased in a foreign currency, (3) creating acceptances, and (4) advancing funds necessary to pay drafts submitted under letters of credit.
The services offered exporters are (1) collecting drafts drawn on foreign importers, (2) advancing funds against drafts pending collection abroad, (3) paying drafts drawn under letters of credit in their favor, and (4) rendering reports on the credit standing of buyers in foreign countries and submitting reports on market conditions and import and export regulations abroad (*North Carolina State Ports,* Summer, 1960, p. 13).

ever, because private firms the Authority was trying to interest in operating it believed there was not sufficient ship and overhaul business to justify the risk. The Navy agreed to move the dock if the state promised to maintain it. The Authority considered moving it and placing it on a standby basis, but at the time was unable to find the funds to maintain and insure it as the Navy required. The cost of insurance was $25,000 a year, and Col. Gillette estimated that from $200,000 to $250,000 would be required to place the dock in operation and that $15,000 a year would be necessary for maintenance. Funds were not available without legislative action.

Another aspect of service is the manner in which the port managements and personnel do their work in handling cargoes. Many statements of praise have been made by shippers and receivers of cargoes and by ship operators about the care, efficiency, and speed with which these operations proceed. The port officials emphasize the personalized service which relatively small, modern ports, such as State Docks and Ocean Terminals, are prepared to offer.

The federal Customs Service is also important in the operations of a seaport. When entering a port the master of a ship must make formal entry of his ship in the marine division of this service by paying a tonnage tax and navigation fees and meeting other requirements, and after the cargo is discharged the ship must be cleared for the next port. Other Customs personnel co-operate with shipping agents and freight forwarders to speed the movement of cargo through a port. Both of the state terminals have efficient Customs service.

After the two new terminals had been completed, the next task was to encourage shippers to use them. To do this the Authority first had to work for competitive advantages for the ports and then to inform shippers of these advantages. This task required time. For almost a decade after the Authority was established, shippers showed little interest in using the ports. This lack of interest was due, among other things, to (1) unfavorable freight rates, which are treated in the following chapter and which have gradually been removed, (2) the lack of regular and dependable sailing schedules from the ports, which also has been overcome to some extent, and (3) the lack of knowledge of the ports on the part of potential shippers. The problems associated with overcoming these obstacles comprise the subject matter of the following chapter.

4. North Carolina State Ports: Trade Territories, Transporation Relationships, and Promotional Activities

Foreign commerce is important to the economy of North Carolina. The state produces both agricultural and industrial commodities for export, and many of its manufacturing enterprises depend upon imported raw materials. E. E. Schnellbacker of the United States Department of Commerce estimated North Carolina's share of the nation's foreign trade in 1960 at a half billion dollars, consisting of $375 million in exports and $125 million in imports, with more than 350 firms participating. Charlotte had a stake of $27 million in this trade.[1] Of course, not all of the state's foreign trade used North Carolina seaports. Executive Director Williams stated that, according to reports of the United States Department of Commerce, North Carolina's seaports in 1959 handled cargoes in foreign trade valued at $184,500,000. Export cargoes were valued at $89,100,000 and import cargoes at $95,400,000. Corresponding figures for 1958 were $87,000,000 and $63,300,000.[2] On this matter a study by the United States Department of State comments: "there is factual evidence which indicates that exports play an important part in the industrial prosperity of the State and are responsible for the employment of several thousands of workers in high-wage industries."[3]

Table 4 shows that the North Carolina seaports are not obtaining what is apparently their competitive share of the deep-water commerce (foreign and coastwise) of the state's industries and commercial establishments. North Carolina ranks fairly high in most of the items in the table except deep-water commerce, in which it ranks lowest.

North Carolina ports have this low relative rank because they are by-passed by patterns of trade that have prevailed for years and are thus difficult to change. According to one study, these patterns are

[1] In an address at the Conference on World Affairs held in Chapel Hill, N. C., Feb. 11-12, 1960 (quoted in *North Carolina State Ports,* Spring, 1960, pp. 10-11).
[2] *North Carolina State Ports,* Spring, 1960, p. 16.
[3] *North Carolina and Foreign Trade* (Washington, D. C., 1951), p. 1.

less efficient and less economical for most receivers and shippers of deep-water trade in the state than is service through the North Carolina ports.   Usually traffic "will use the nearest and most convenient port at which adequate services and facilities are provided,"[4] but when, as in the case of the North Carolina seaports, unfavorable patterns of trade become established, "Far more shippers and receivers of freight are motivated in their routings by tradition, friendship and lethargy, than by a continuing attention to the most economical routings."[5]   The patterns of trade that have become established may be accounted for by natural and historical influences.

Certain features of the state's physical geography have prevented good transportation relationships.   The nature of the coastline and the mountain barrier in the west have combined their effects to cause a north-south development of railroad routes in the state.   The poor location of North Carolina for the growth of important seaports was recognized by the original colonists and has been complained about ever since.

The seaward extension of the state relative to neighboring states and the east-west trend of the coast south of Cape Hatteras influence the tributary areas of the state's ports, and hence of their competitors'. Based on distance, these factors place the southwestern quarter of the state in the Charleston trade area and a strip of the northeastern corner in the Norfolk trade area.   Both of these are productive areas.   Conversely, a portion of northeastern South Carolina and southwestern Virginia are in the Wilmington trade area.   These peculiar features

[4] Buckley Report, p. 68.
[5] Ibid., pp. 68-69.

Table 4. Per Capita Figures for Selected Items for the United States, North Carolina, Virginia, South Carolina, and Georgia, 1959

State	Per Capita				
	Farm Value of Crops Sold (dollars)	Value Added by Manufacture[a] (dollars)	Retail Sales[a] (dollars)	Wholesale Sales[a] (dollars)	Deep-Water Commerce (tons)
United States	108	816	1,148	1,620	3.0
North Carolina	163	689	859	1,125	0.91
Virginia	102	545	953	893	10.46[b]
South Carolina	113	569	731	671	1.74
Georgia	97	816	932	1,512	1.10

[a] 1958.
[b] Hampton Roads.
Source: Statistical Abstract of the United States.

of the coastline also place North Carolina ports at some distance from the major ocean route along the country's east coast.

The dangerous nature of the North Carolina coast has been another obstacle to the growth of ports. Offshore shoals and shallow river entrances make the waters dangerous and difficult for ships to navigate. Deep, narrow channels have been dredged and are kept clear, but such activities are costly.

The mountains in western North Carolina, by making contact difficult with the productive interior plains, have prevented volume movements of east-west freight or of bulk freight from the Midwest to North Carolina ports for export.

The north-south rail routes that developed had important terminals at Charleston and Norfolk. The establishment of freight rates favoring these out-of-state ports encouraged North Carolina shippers to use them, restricting the trade areas of the North Carolina ports still more. Trade became well established in this pattern.

Adjustments gradually have been made in the unfavorable rail rates and recently Executive Director Williams stated, "I believe we have corrected every instance of discrimination that we know about."[6] The state terminals even had local discriminations with which to contend. Switching charges were a problem at first at both ports. For example, at one time at State Docks a charge of $22.71 was made to switch a car of fertilizer from the docks to plants in the local area, whereas the charge was only $12.01 from the other docks at Wilmington.[7]

Trade Territories of the Carolina Ports

There are two schools of thought regarding the requirements for successful port development. One school holds that the hinterland, combined with the transportation facilities linking it to the port, is of primary importance. The other school believes that the hinterland is of secondary importance and that factors such as location of the port with respect to sea routes, terminal facilities, and services for handling traffic are of first importance.[8]

[6] Quoted in Davis, *op. cit.,* D:1.
[7] "The Ports Problem," *The State,* May 2, 1953, p. 4.
[8] See G. G. Weigand, "Ports: Their Hinterlands and Forelands," *The Geographical Review,* XLII (1952), 661-662.

Both concepts may have validity, depending upon the location and stage of development of a particular port. If there are no port facilities, obviously, traffic cannot be attracted; and if there is no traffic, private enterprise cannot afford to construct terminals; and even if there is potential traffic the period of development may be too long for private investment to be attracted. But after the volume of traffic has permitted the port to reach a stage of development in which it is well supplied with terminal facilities and services and there are frequent shipping schedules, these influences act as a magnet to draw still more commerce to the port.

A port's hinterland consists of (1) a tributary area for which the port is the natural outlet because of low transportation costs, and (2) a competitive territory which is sufficiently distant that freight costs to other ports influence the shipper.

For most ports the major source of trade is likely to be in the competitive territory. For the North Carolina state ports, however, most of the commerce for some time will be with the area for which the particular port is the natural outlet. The Buckley Report reveals that the traffic of these ports moved largely to and from the adjacent trade area, and states that the future of the ports will depend largely upon the recapture of traffic from this territory that now moves through competing ports.[9]

In 1957 the trade territory of Morehead City contained twenty-one counties and that of Wilmington sixty-nine counties. Morehead City was the natural outlet for nine counties and the port competed with Norfolk and Wilmington in the other counties. In seven of these counties the freight rate was lower than the Wilmington rate and equal to the Norfolk rate and in four the rate was lower than the Norfolk and equal to the Wilmington rate. In one county the rate was the same to all three ports.

The trade territory of Wilmington was comprised of fifty counties in North Carolina, nine in South Carolina, four in Tennessee, three in Kentucky, and three in Virginia. The exclusive territory included all or part of forty-five counties in North Carolina and six counties in South Carolina. In all or part of four other North Carolina counties the rate was equal to that for Morehead City but lower than the rate to competitive ports. In part of one North Carolina county the rate was the same as the rate to Wilmington and to Norfolk. In the remain-

[9] Pp. 68, 88.

ing part of the competitive territory the rate was lower than that to Morehead City and equal to that to competing ports.[10]

The principal trade territory, thus, is seen to lie within the state. The importance of these ports to the commerce of a large tributary area suggests that the ports are in a large degree a matter of state-wide interest. Emphasized also is the importance to the economy of the state of recapturing commerce now moving through other ports—traffic which moves through other ports because of trade channels developed when North Carolina ports lacked modern facilities and favorable freight rates.

Wilmington and Morehead City also hold a competitive position with North Atlantic and Gulf ports over a section of the Midwest, including all or part of ten states in Official and Western Trunk Line rate territories. Regardless of competitive freight rates, however, North Carolina ports cannot expect to attract much tonnage from the Midwest. Present trade patterns for this traffic are firmly established, and North Carolina ports do not have any advantages over other ports in handling it.

A primary requirement for the growth of a seaport is favorable railway relationships with a large territory which serves both as a source of traffic for exports and as a market for imports. Good railway relationships include such matters as modern physical facilities, favorable competitive rate relationships, a major railway route or routes or else interline agreements which will funnel and draw commerce into the port. "A main railroad network having a single port outlet acts as a powerful solicitor for a port. Indeed, railway solicitation is often well-organized, far-flung, and relatively more effective than official port promotion in attracting traffic through a port."[11] Each railroad makes rates which will attract tonnage to the port it serves. The development of the port at Charleston has been due largely to the enterprise of railroads, and the same is probably true of Norfolk.

Wilmington is served by two trunk-line railroad companies, Morehead City, until recently, by only a short-line railroad. Wilmington does not possess an east-west trunk-line contact with areas which can

[10] For a discussion and maps of these trade territories, see the Buckley Report, pp. 89-91, 102-103.

[11] D. J. Patton, "General Cargo Hinterlands of New York, Philadelphia, Baltimore, and New Orleans," *Annals of the Association of American Geographers,* XLVIII (1958), 453.

ship to it in competition with Norfolk, Charleston, and Savannah the necessary bulk-cargo to make it a port of frequent sailings for satisfactory service.[12]

Furthermore, the city is served by a branch line of the Seaboard Air Line, and it is only an intermediate point on the Atlantic Coast Line.   Since a railroad does not care to short-haul itself, most of the north-south rail traffic bypasses Wilmington.   For example, if a shipment for New York is picked up at Charleston or Atlanta, the railroad receives more revenue by hauling it as far as it can, and therefore does not care to leave it at some intermediate point for water movement.

The short line between Goldsboro and Morehead City, the Atlantic and East Carolina Railroad, was purchased by the Southern Railway in 1957 for $527,000.[13]   This acquisition also included a spur from Havelock to the Cherry Point base.   This short line interchanges traffic with the Norfolk-Southern at New Bern, Kinston, and Goldsboro, and it meets the Southern Railway at Goldsboro and the Camp Lejeune Railroad at Havelock.   The purchase of the Atlantic and East Caro-

[12] The Cape Fear and Yadkin Valley Railroad, connecting Wilmington and Mt. Airy, represented an effort in the early nineteenth century to connect the Midwest and tidewater in North Carolina.   But before the line could secure a connection or be built into the Midwest it was forced into bankruptcy by rival interests, and was bought and dismembered.

Later, in 1852, the Western Railroad was chartered to connect mineral deposits of the Deep River section in Moore and Chatham counties with navigable water on the Cape Fear River.   The railroad, its name having been changed to the Cape Fear and Yadkin Valley Railway Company in 1879, was gradually expanded until it reached Mt. Airy in 1889 and Wilmington in 1890.   Plans were made for a connection with the Norfolk and Western Railroad which would have made a trunk line from Cincinnati to Wilmington, and the shortest line between the Midwest and South Atlantic ports. The Norfolk and Western planned to instal "Virginia Cities Gateway" rates, which would have placed the North Carolina line in a favorable position to develop the port of Wilmington.   But these rates never became effective.   They were opposed by the Richmond and Danville Railroad (now a part of Southern Railway), and to prevent their establishment that railroad gave the Norfolk and Western favorable traffic concessions and permission to solicit traffic in its territory.   The foregoing is an interesting bit of economic history one should recall when he reads that high railroad rates in North Carolina have been the natural result of the operation of economic laws in the railroad field.

In the panic of 1893 the Cape Fear and Yadkin Valley Railway Company went into receivership.   The receivership lasted five years, after which the company was bought jointly by the Atlantic Coast Line (then the Wilmington and Weldon Railroad) and the Southern Railway, and ultimately was divided between them.   (For an account of the history of these early railroads in North Carolina, see *Report of the State Ship and Water Transportation Commission* [Raleigh, N. C., 1924], pp. 18, 118-121.)

[13] The Atlantic and East Carolina Railroad Company is a privately owned operating company.   The right of way and structures are owned by the Atlantic and North Carolina Railroad Company, in which the State of North Carolina is the principal stockholder.   The Southern Railway leases the latter company.

lina Railroad by the Southern Railway provides Morehead City with physical trunk-line service with the thirteen states served by the Southern, but it remains to be seen whether traffic can be attracted in volume from the Midwest. Favorable freight rates as well as the physical connections are necessary for the development of traffic. At present the freight yards at Morehead City are not adequate for caring for a heavy movement of freight through the port.

In 1961 the Interstate Commerce Commission approved the acquisition of the Camp Lejeune Railroad Company by the Southern Railway. The former company was authorized to issue 1,000 shares of no par common stock to the Southern Railway to obtain working capital. At the same time the Camp Lejeune Railroad and the Atlantic Coast Line Railroad were permitted to operate over separate sections of the Marine Corps Railroad (owned by the federal government) from Havelock to Jacksonville, N. C., through the Camp Lejeune Marine Base, and to operate certain other lines jointly.

In acquiring the Atlantic and East Carolina Railroad the Southern Railway made it understood that it would co-operate with development agencies in the area to develop Morehead City further as a port and to encourage new industry to locate in the hinterland of Morehead City.[14] Shortly after acquiring this short line the Southern took steps to stimulate commerce at the port. Early in 1959 competitive freight rates were established on commodities moving to and from Morehead City. Other ports, particularly Wilmington, opposed these new rates, but in June, 1961, an Interstate Commerce Commission examiner ruled that the public interest would be better served by equalization of the export-import rates at Morehead City with the lower rates in effect at Wilmington.[15]

In the summer of 1961 the Southern announced multiple-car rates on grain from Ohio and Mississippi river points to points in the Southeast served by that railway. There were objections to these rates and they have been suspended while the Interstate Commerce Commission investigates them. If allowed to go into effect, such rates may attract midwestern grain shipments to Morehead City.

Four U. S. interstate highways, including Route 17, the coastal route between the Northeast and Florida, serve Wilmington. These

[14] See "Partners in Progress at Morehead City, North Carolina," in *Ties,* the *Southern Railway System Magazine,* Dec., 1960, p. 15.
[15] *Ties,* July, 1961, p. 2.

permit service to Wilmington as an intermediate point in through north and south motor carrier service, as well as originating and terminating trips throughout its hinterland. Morehead City lies east of the main north-south flow of traffic and is reached by only a single U. S. interstate highway (Route 70). These railway and highway connections are important for stimulating trade because not much of the new traffic hoped for will originate or terminate at the port cities. Both cities are also located on the route of the Intracoastal Waterway, and Wilmington is served by the Cape Fear River and its tributaries.

Table 5 indicates the number of railroad cars and trucks receiving or discharging cargo at the two state terminals annually. Recently the annual growth in the number of both types of conveyance has been marked at State Docks. Ocean Terminals shows a growth in truck traffic, but the number of railroad cars has remained steady.

Table 5. Number of Railroad Cars and Trucks Receiving or Discharging Cargo at the Two State Ports

Year	State Docks		Ocean Terminals	
	Railroad Cars	Trucks	Railroad Cars	Trucks
1952	a	a	a	a
1953	a	a	a	a
1954	a	a	a	a
1955	2,888	1,924	a	a
1956	1,936	2,855	a	a
1957	2,901	3,195	a	a
1958	3,433	2,702	849	1,997
1959	4,392	5,204	907	3,146
1960	5,505	6,493	899	3,106

ᵃ No record.
Source: Material furnished by the State Ports Authority.

Existing railway arrangements make possible the distribution of water-borne products from both ports throughout North Carolina, northern South Carolina, and eastern Tennessee. But there is also a territory for competitive ocean traffic extending into the Midwest which might be tapped by a trunk route or even by means of interchange connection and agreements. Such arrangements also might result in coal moving from the middle Appalachian coal field to these ports for the export and coast-wise trades. It is difficult, however, to induce a railroad to divert traffic from ports where it has made a heavy investment in terminal facilities, and the railroads that might help the Carolina ports all have heavy investments in ports elsewhere.

In testimony at hearings which the Interstate Commerce Commission held on the proposal, Director Ben E. Douglas of the Department of Conservation and Development believed that the acquisition of the Atlantic and East Carolina by the Southern would overcome this handicap under which the ports operate. Among other advantages, Director Douglas said that such an arrangement would lead to better service at lower rates between coastal North Carolina and the Midwest, and would assist in developing traffic for the state port at Morehead City, as well as encouraging the industrial development of the agricultural eastern part of the state.[16]

Another aspect of transportation is the availability of vessel space as it is needed. In the past, ships of the same companies called at both Morehead City and Wilmington. Regular schedules were not maintained. Ships called if a sufficient quantity of cargo was offered to make the call profitable. Such service was deemed adequate for the type and quantity of cargo offered. Ships do not care to make regular calls at a port unless it can supply a dependable and sufficient supply of cargo. Adding a new port of call adds three or more days to a ship's operating costs, which amount to $3,000 or more per day and continue whether the ship is docked or moving.

During the past several years several ocean lines have established regular schedules for the foreign trade. The amount of such services, though, is inadequate compared with other South Atlantic ports. A greater frequency and variety of deep-water services are necessary for North Carolina ports.

Late in 1954 the Isthmian Steamship Company announced that it was making Wilmington the first port of call for its ships arriving from India, Pakistan, and Egypt with cargoes of jute, jute products, and Egyptian cotton. In 1958 this company established regularly scheduled outward sailings from Wilmington in its Mediterranean–Ceylon service, which included ports of the Near East and India and the port of Colombo. This company therefore operates both an inward and an outward service at Wilmington.

In January, 1955, the South Atlantic Steamship Line, Inc., of Savannah, Georgia (a division of United States Lines), inaugurated regular monthly services westbound from Europe to Wilmington without minimum cargo guarantees. This service was possible because of the greatly increased variety and volume of shipments carried

[16] *Durham Morning Herald,* June 11, 1955, 1:7.

by the vessels of that firm during the preceding year. Wilmington is the first port of discharge, and is followed by Charleston, Savannah, and Jacksonville. The sailings are from Antwerp, with calls at other ports of northwestern Europe. The principal products brought in are steel, hardware, burlap, fertilizer, cocoa extract, and bicycles, mostly for distribution in North Carolina. For eastbound service to Europe this company makes frequent calls as cargo offers. Outbound cargo consists chiefly of wood pulp, tobacco, and forest products.[17]

In late 1956 the United States Lines announced a new service with monthly schedules to bring to Wilmington cargoes loaded at Manchester and Liverpool and with calls at Glasgow and at Dublin as cargoes were offered. Wilmington was listed as the first port of call. Chemicals, machinery, and steel products are the principal articles in this trade. The direct shipment saves time and thus reduces insurance charges. There is also the convenience of receiving the cargo quickly.[18] In 1958 this company announced monthly schedules from North Sea ports to Wilmington.

In the summer of 1957 the Holland-American Line announced monthly schedules from Morehead City to the north European ports of Antwerp, Rotterdam, Hamburg, and Bremen. This service was the first regular one to be established from Morehead City. Tobacco was the principal item of traffic. Tobacco is considered to be an ideal cargo by ship operators. The hogsheads can be loaded to use space efficiently, and there is little chance of the cargo shifting on the rolling oceans. At about the same time two new services for Wilmington were announced. The Royal Netherlands Steamship Company began a regular biweekly service between Wilmington and several ports in the Caribbean islands and Venezuela,[19] and the Manchester Lines, Ltd., established biweekly schedules between Wilmington and the British ports of Manchester and Liverpool. At Wilmington general cargo, chiefly tobacco, is loaded and the ships return to Wilmington with general cargo.

In 1958 the Daido Line began a monthly service outward between Wilmington and the Far Eastern ports of Manila, Hong Kong, Keelung, and the major Japanese ports. In the same year the Ozean-

[17] *North Carolina State Ports,* Fall, 1955, p. 19.
[18] *Ibid.,* Dec., 1956, p. 13.
[19] *Ibid.,* June, 1957, p. 16.

Stinnes Line announced biweekly sailings from Hamburg, Bremen, Rotterdam, and Antwerp to the North Carolina ports and other South Atlantic ports, and the Mamenic Line of the International Shipping Company announced a monthly service from Wilmington.[20]

Early in 1959 the Waterman Steamship Corporation announced monthly schedules inward between Wilmington and Far Eastern ports in Korea, Japan, and Formosa.[21]   In the fall of that year the American Export Lines began service between the two state ports and the principal ports of Portugal, Spain, and the northern shore of the Mediterranean, and in February, 1960, established service between Wilmington and the principal ports of Italy and Yugoslavia.   The vessels in the latter service are equipped to handle refrigerated cargo. In the former service the cargo liner schedules established should be a convenience to southern buyers of tobacco from Greece and Turkey.[22] The first cargo of Turkish tobacco imported through a North Carolina port arrived at Wilmington early in 1960.

In the summer of 1960 the Splosna Plavba Line of Piran, Yugoslavia, announced monthly sailings from Wilmington, linking that port with the Mediterranean ports of Tangier, Naples, and Genoa, and the ports of Trieste and Rijeka.[23]

Many other ships than those operating on regular schedules call at the state ports, and with the increase in volume and variety of cargo they call more frequently than in the past.

The Norfolk, Baltimore, and Carolina Line operates a weekly package service connecting Charleston, Wilmington, Norfolk, Baltimore, and points on the Intracoastal Waterway between these ports. The traffic consists of numerous articles that are in common use in the hinterlands of the ports.   Movement inland by truck may be 150 miles or more.[24]

Port cities have a direct interest in the call of a ship because of the money spent by its owner in docking, loading, unloading, and servicing the ship, as well as that spent by the ship's personnel in the business establishments of the city.   Officials of the Authority esti-

[20] *Ibid.*, Jan., 1959, p. 3.
[21] *Ibid.*, April, 1959, p. 16.
[22] *Ibid.*, Nov., 1959, p. 15.
[23] *Ibid.*, Summer, 1960, p. 17.
[24] *The Ports of Wilmington and Morehead City, North Carolina,* Port Series No. 12 (revised 1950), Corps of Engineers, Department of the Army and Maritime Commission, U. S. Department of Commerce, Washington, D. C., 1951, pp. 56-57. This same source on p. 135 states that there are semi-weekly schedules.

mated in 1958 that each ship that calls leaves behind $10,000 for such items as the purchase of provisions and fuel, laundry, tug boat charges, and wharfage and dockage. There is also additional revenue from stevedoring costs, agents' fees, insurance, inland freight rates, and so forth.

Following are the expenses of a representative freighter (7,000 tons) calling at Wilmington to discharge a load of fertilizer as given in a statement of the Authority on March 4, 1954:

Tonnage dues	$ 271.20
Entering Customs	2.70
Clearing Customs	2.00
Boarding ship	9.52
Immigration	9.52
Running lines	40.00
Harbor master	15.00
Notary public	5.00
Overtime, warehousemen	116.00
Overtime, stevedores	249.84
Time lost	306.99
Stevedoring	16,482.50
Harbor charges	780.00
Pilotage	230.00
Postage and petties	20.00
Agency fees	250.00
Long distance calls	61.73
Telegrams	25.84
Ship chandlers	11.52
Water	101.50
Doctors	136.50
Laundry	132.50
Repairs	275.00
Medicines	23.75
Cash advanced to master for crew	14,000.00
Total	**$33,558.61**

An export cargo of cottonseed meal was estimated to have brought the following revenues to the port area: $40,000 to the railroads that delivered the shipment to the port; $20,000 to stevedores; $10,000 to terminal operators for handling in transit sheds; $5,000 to freight forwarders, steamship agents, and insurance companies.

These figures amount to a total of $75,000, and it was estimated that a similar quantity of products that were more valuable per unit than cottonseed meal could bring in as much as $125,000 in revenue to the port area.[25]

[25] *North Carolina State Ports,* Fall, 1958, p. 5.

Educational and Promotional Activities

From the beginning the State Ports Authority has conducted a program of activities designed to inform shippers and the public about the activities and progress of the state terminals, and about the advantages both to shippers and the economy of the state in using these terminals. This program is under the supervision of the Director of Public Relations. Many different means are employed in conducting these activities. Included are the official publication of the Authority, namely, *North Carolina State Ports,* news releases, television and radio programs and announcements, addresses by members of the board and by operating officials, the employment of the traffic solicitors mentioned above, and trade missions to various parts of the United States and to foreign countries, although these missions have not been for the sole purpose of advertising the state ports.

The official publication of the Authority gives news about the activities and progress of the ports and now has a section called "Trade Leads" which lists the export opportunities for the different products of the state in different foreign countries, and import opportunities in the state for foreign goods. The executive director, as well as other officials, addresses many kinds of organizations, including engineering societies, traffic organizations, trade associations, and civic and professional clubs.

In the middle 1950's, as a result of experience and knowledge gained regarding sources of traffic, the solicitation program was expanded and concentrated more on the likely items of traffic. Whether there is any connection between this shift in emphasis and the volume of traffic is not known, but, at any rate, the number of the items of traffic and the volume both have increased since the change was introduced. In 1960 the types of commodities numbered more than 300. In 1961 the Authority had more than 500 shippers. Between 15 and 20 per cent of them were from the Charlotte area.

The solicitation and development of particular items of traffic in volume usually has been a time-consuming process. Usually there are many different sides to a problem of this sort and each one has to be given consideration. A great deal of correspondence must take place between the Authority and the different interests involved. These activities, in connection with tobacco and lumber from the

Pacific Northwest, are outlined in the following chapter. Other examples of products which have been solicited with some success are condensed and powdered milk and cotton textiles. The files of the Authority in the State Department of Archives and History contain a voluminous correspondence on these products and others as well.

Opinions differ as to the sources of new traffic for the state terminals. The Buckley Report states that the future of the ports is not dependent on a substantial growth in deep-water trade but upon the provision of facilities to accommodate the traffic which should use these ports from the standpoint of economic advantage.[26] This statement refers primarily to the recapture of traffic now going to competing ports but certainly includes any new traffic which should use the North Carolina ports for the same reason.

Mr. Schnellbacker of the U.S. Commerce Department believed the state's foreign trade potential would be found in newer industries rather than in those historically important, with one exception. He did think that prospects were good for increasing textile exports because the industry had not been aggressive in developing world markets for its products.[27] Executive Director Williams seemed to agree with Mr. Schnellbacker. Mr. Williams credited much of the growth in traffic to the steady expansion of industry in North Carolina.[28]

In 1960 the Authority had a comprehensive study made to determine how much ocean shipping the state can support and to find out what to expect in growth potential at the two ports. The information assembled was to provide the basis for the request for funds the Authority planned to seek from the 1961 General Assembly. In July, 1960, the Advisory Budget Commission was asked for $13,500,000 in capital improvements to add to berthing facilities and to increase the warehousing space and the industrial site potential. The Commission approved this request.[29]

The Trade and Industries mission led by Governor Hodges to Western Europe and England in November, 1959, was sponsored jointly by the State Ports Authority and the Department of Conservation and Development. Nine Tarheel industrial and business leaders

[26] P. 4.
[27] *North Carolina State Ports,* Spring, 1960, p. 16.
[28] *Ibid.,* Nov., 1959, p. 2.
[29] Bruce, *op. cit.*

and three members of the Authority, individually and in groups, made return or follow-up trips to renew contacts and build more good will.[30]

On this mission Governor Hodges pushed both the North Carolina seaports and the state's advantages for the investment of capital in industry. One example from this trip illustrates one type of problem faced by a small but developing seaport. In Zurich the Governor met an exporter of textile machinery who, in spite of the fact that 75 per cent of his sales in this country were to customers in North Carolina, maintained an agent and a warehouse in New York City. This exporter did not know that the state had seaports.[31]

After the officials returned from Europe, the Authority began to place new emphasis on industrial development in the areas adjacent to the two ports, with particular attention being given to European contacts made on the good-will tour. The trade fair, held by the State of North Carolina at Charlotte in the fall of 1961, had the same general objective that the trade mission had.

Another organization which tries to encourage exports is the North Carolina Regional Export Expansion Committee. In 1960 the United States Department of Commerce sponsored the organization of the National Export Expansion Committee and thirty-three regional expansion committees. The committee members are leading men in industry and business. The function of the regional committees is to inform industry of export opportunities and of the need for expanding the national economy. In furthering these objectives, these committees work with banks and chambers of commerce and sponsor regional export conferences and special meetings. The North Carolina Re-

[30] *North Carolina State Ports,* Spring, 1960, p. 6.
[31] "Carolina Woos the Rich European," *Business Week,* Nov. 21, 1959, p. 144.

Table 6. Average Annual Tonnages of Waterborne Freight Traffic by Five-Year Periods, 1931-1960 at Norfolk, Charleston, Savannah, and Wilmington (in thousands)[a]

Year	Norfolk	Charleston	Savannah	Wilmington
1931-35	12,890	1,856	2,491	1,160
1936-40	19,088	2,387	3,573	2,135
1946-50	21,718	4,025	2,826	2,640
1951-55	30,397	4,120	3,777	3,573
1956-60	40,844	4,441	4,192	4,932

[a] The war period, 1941-45, is omitted.
Source: See source to Table 7.

gional Export Committee is aiding in promoting and organizing the trade fair mentioned above.

Table 6 indicates that efforts to make North Carolina's seaports more economical and convenient for shippers to use and to promote their use have had results insofar as Wilmington and its chief competitor, Charleston, are concerned. Table 17 in Chapter 6 shows a similar situation in regard to Morehead City and Norfolk.

5. The Volume of Commerce of the State Ports

The total commerce of the seaports of Wilmington and Morehead City for the past thirty years and that of the state terminals at both cities since beginning operations are shown in Table 7. The total tonnages for the two seaports reveal their growth and provide a comparison of the relative importance of the state port at each city. One should bear in mind that the state terminals were established largely to accommodate types of traffic that the older port facilities were inadequate to handle. Furthermore, the diversity of the products handled by the state ports is greater and their value per unit is higher than of those handled by the other port facilities. For these reasons, a direct comparison of tonnages alone may not show the full importance of the state terminals.

The tonnage at all major United States ports is dominated by bulk commodities, and petroleum is a leading item of traffic for all but a few of the coastal ports. The hinterlands of the North Carolina ports absorb substantial quantities of bulk freight, chiefly petroleum products, but they do not produce large quantities of cheap bulk articles that seek low-cost water transportation. Most of the commodities for export fall into the package freight classification, but vessels need bulk freight, not much of which is available for export from North Carolina and none enters into coastwise shipments. Neither do the ports attract large quantities of package import freight needed by Carolina industry, one reason being that the principal bulk item imported, petroleum, is transported in specialized vessels and originates in areas that do not have package freight to export.[1]

Package freight is not usually loaded as a ship's entire load but rather is "topping" for a cargo, and usually seeks the nearest busy port. There schedules are frequent and competition brings prompt shipment and low freight rates.

[1] For more details on this subject, see B. E. Logan, "An Historical Geographic Study of North Carolina Ports." Unpublished Ph.D. dissertation, University of North Carolina, 1956; also, S. T. Emory, "North Carolina Ports," *The State,* Nov. 25, 1944. p. 18.

Because general cargo is hauled in this manner, at Wilmington State Docks, handling general cargo, and private docks, handling chiefly dry bulk cargo, supplement each other. This condition should increase the attractiveness of Wilmington as a port of call for ships. The same situation does not exist at Morehead City. There the Authority owns all of the general and dry bulk cargo facilities, and most of the bulk cargo is liquid cargo which moves in specialized vessels.

Table 7 shows more tonnage at the state terminals at Morehead City than at the corresponding facility at Wilmington, although the total traffic at the port of Wilmington is much the greater of the two. Almost all of the commercial traffic at Morehead City is handled on the property of the State Ports Authority, whereas at Wilmington the major portion moves over privately owned terminal facilities. A large proportion of the traffic at Morehead City consists of petroleum products. Wilmington has a much heavier traffic in petroleum products, but there the oil companies have their own terminal facilities. At Morehead City directly opposite from the state dock a major

Table 7. Commerce of the Ports of Wilmington, Morehead City Harbor, and the State Terminals

	Tons			
	Wilmington		Morehead City Harbor	
Year	Total	State Docks	Total	Ocean Terminals[c]
1931-35	1,159,791[a]	—	8,137[a]	—
1936-40	2,134,664[a]	—	104,723[a]	—
1941-45	1,107,600[a]	—	18,987[a]	—
1946-51	2,854,594[b]	—	226,884[b]	—
1952	3,428,498	23,498	455,742	366,817
1953	3,301,786	96,153	536,685	437,151
1954	3,426,564	104,837	504,205	358,043
1955	3,781,702	250,793	446,655	299,171
1956	3,812,584	278,583	479,320	317,461
1957	3,588,648	306,175	453,794	316,403
1958	3,859,411	184,457	506,616	354,154
1959	4,142,279	284,056	574,706	378,309
1960	4,179,751	352,271	678,986	382,381

[a] 5-year average.
[b] 6-year average.
[c] Does not include military traffic.

Source: For total tonnages, Annual Reports, Chief of Engineers, U. S. Army, prior to 1953; Waterborne Commerce of the United States, Part 1 (Annual), Corps of Engineers, Department of the Army, since 1952; for state terminals, material supplied by the State Ports Authority. The traffic statistics in Chaps. 5 and 6 are for the calendar year.

petroleum company operates a private terminal for high-test aviation gasoline and jet fuel that is used at the Cherry Point Air Base.

Table 8 indicates the number of commercial ships which made calls at the state terminals each year. Not every one of these ships called to deliver or load cargo. Some of them were visitors and a few stopped for water. Military vessels which bring in revenue are also handled at Morehead City. The number has ranged from 139 in 1956 to 251 in 1960.

Table 8. Number of Commercial Ships Calling at the State Terminals at Morehead City and Wilmington

Year	Morehead City	Wilmington
1952	—	16
1953	51	45
1954	62	73
1955	50	115
1956	37	113
1957	58	171
1958	129	216
1959	97	254
1960	169	377

Morehead City Harbor

Table 9 provides a summary of the traffic at Morehead City Harbor and shows the distribution of the tonnage at Ocean Terminals among broad classes of traffic. Although liquid cargo and military cargo provide revenue for the Authority, so far as port development is concerned dry cargo is the important class of traffic. Its growth in quantity and diversity indicates the extent to which industry and business in the state are patronizing the port. The growth in quantity thus far is not outstanding and leaf tobacco provides a large proportion of the total tonnage. The Authority hopes to develop commerce in grain at Ocean Terminals.

Table 10 classifies the tonnage at Morehead City Harbor on the basis of the kind of movement, whether foreign, coastwise, internal, or local, beginning with 1936. This table shows that Morehead City had a substantial tonnage before the state port was constructed. Petroleum products comprise a large part of the imports, coastwise receipts, and

internal shipments.   The latter represent a distribution of a portion
of the tonnages of the other two types of movement.   Local tonnage
consists largely of the products of the fishery industry.   The facilities
for receiving seafoods are all on Bogue Sound, and each one has
buildings for processing and packing and facilities for shipping to
interior points in the Carolinas and Virginia and to the large northern
cities.   Fresh fish and other seafoods move by refrigerated trucks.
This table indicates the kinds of traffic movements at Ocean Terminals
because that facility now handles a large part of the total tonnage
at Morehead City Harbor.

The secret of port growth at Morehead City is the location of two
United States military bases nearby (Camp Lejeune and Cherry Point
Air Base).   These installations use large quantities of refined petroleum, a portion of which is unloaded from the tankers by use of the
facilities of Ocean Terminals.   Furthermore, the presence of these
military bases has caused more harbor improvements than would have
been made otherwise.

In 1952 two of the new warehouses at Ocean Terminals were
leased to the United States Navy for a sum of $43,325 annually. These
warehouses were used for storing supplies for the two military bases.
They had been built for the storage of export tobacco leaf, but were
leased to the Navy because of its urgent need for the best type of shipside storage and transit services and because the Authority had no
need for the capacity at the time. However, the Navy no longer leases

Table 9. Tonnages of Traffic at Morehead City Harbor and Ocean Terminals
and of Classes of Traffic at Ocean Terminals

	Commercial Tonnage[a]		Ocean Terminals			
Year	Morehead City Harbor	Ocean Terminals	Dry Cargo	Liquid Cargo	Military	Total[b]
1952	455,742	366,817	0	366,817	37,223	404,040
1953	536,685	437,152	29,416	407,736	87,954	525,106
1954	504,205	360,273	6,180	354,093	210,905	571,178
1955	446,655	299,171	6,800	292,371	187,144	486,315
1956	479,320	317,461	41,204	276,257	93,623	411,084
1957	453,794	316,403	29,629	286,774	93,203	409,606
1958	506,616	354,154	45,925	308,229	133,523	487,677
1959	574,706	378,309	69,612	308,697	69,571	447,880
1960	678,986	382,381	74,801	307,580	125,223	507,604

[a] The difference between the two columns beneath is the tonnage handled by private facilities
[b] The sum of the preceding three columns.
Source: Materials supplied by the State Ports Authority; also, see source to Table 7.

the two warehouses. It has constructed storage facilities and docking facilities for LST vessels on Radio Island. Other classes of ships are still accommodated at Ocean Terminals. As the traffic of the Authority grew, it needed the warehouses for its own use.

There is revenue from the military account for wharfage and other services. Equipment and supplies are shipped to vessels' on maneuvers and on tours and there is a steady flow of supplies and personnel in through the port to the military camps. Military men have commented on the ease and economy with which large transports are docked and the personnel and cargo dispatched. Three loading ramps which made possible the simultaneous handling of three ships were built to accommodate the Navy LST type of vessel. The military bases near Morehead City use Ocean Terminals as a port of embarkation for military personnel and Fort Bragg uses State Docks for the same purpose.

The Esso Standard Oil Company, the leading supplier of tonnage at Morehead City, leases thirteen acres of land from the Authority on which it has constructed storage facilities, and the Trumbull Asphalt Company leases a small tract on which it has constructed storage tanks. The oil company imports petroleum products for

Table 10. Tonnages of Waterborne Commerce at Morehead City Harbor by Classes of Movement

| | | Foreign | | Domestic | | | | |
| | | | | Coastwise | | Internal | | |
Year	Total	Imports	Exports	Receipts	Shipments	Receipts	Shipments	Local
1936-40[a]	104,723	6,989[b]	[c]	816[d]	[c]	13,892	1,293	—
1941-45[a]	20,987	11,239[f]	[c]	9,006[g]	[c]	9,644	4,056[h]	—
1946-52[e]	259,578	77,075	[c]	139,431	[c]	11,809	27,377	4,559[i]
1953	536,685	141,774	3,041	287,697	3,201	19,088	80,056	1,728
1954	504,205	145,635	4,066	169,210	9,864	60,779	113,567	1,084
1955	446,655	129,029	6,265	163,775	18,203	42,314	85,944	1,128
1956	479,320	87,713	29,898	213,783	13,400	19,735	105,865	8,926
1957	453,794	161,552	27,201	129,889	18,206	21,240	90,961	4,745
1958	506,616	155,720	50,415	143,664	9,477	19,673	120,927	6,740
1959	574,706	161,977	73,312	190,217	14,922	10,776	122,422	1,080
1960	678,986	217,044	77,112	226,768	23,158	26,069	107,659	1,176

[a] 5-year average.
[b] 3-year average, 1938-40.
[c] None recorded in source.
[d] 2-year average, 1936-37.
[e] 7-year average.
[f] 2-year average, 1941-42.
[g] 2-year average, 1942-43.
[h] 4-year average, 1941-44.
[i] 6-year average, 1947-52.
Source: See source of Table 7.

reshipment to interior points and for the fueling facilities it maintains for vessels. The Authority has a contract with the Dow Chemical Company for the storage of glycol, a residue used in making anti-freeze. The glycol is from the DuPont synthetic fiber plant at Kinston. Special tanks and lines have been installed for handling this product and other industrial chemicals through Ocean Terminals. The glycol is sold to Dow by DuPont for shipment in coastwise traffic to Texas City, Texas, where it is refined. Dow also assembles glycol from plants in Ohio and New Jersey at Ocean Terminals for shipment to Texas City.

Recently a privately owned and privately operated terminal with complete facilities for receiving and dispatching high-test aviation and jet fuels was constructed on an eighteen-acre tract leased from the Authority on Radio Island near the Esso Standard Oil tank farm. This new facility has no connection with the Authority but it does increase the traffic in petroleum products in Morehead City Harbor.

Table 11 gives the tonnages of foreign commerce at the Port of Wilmington and at State Docks.[2] The imports of the former are several times those of the latter but the exports at State Docks comprise a large share of the total exports at the Port of Wilmington. Because State Docks is a general cargo terminal, the state terminal handles a large proportion of the exports of general cargo of the entire

[2] The Port of Wilmington includes State Docks.

Table 11. Tonnages of Foreign Commerce at the Port of Wilmington and at State Docks

| Year | Wilmington | | State Docks[a] | |
	Imports	Exports	Imports	Exports
1952	213,651	7,423	22,408	1,090
1953	196,929	21,865[b]	70,320	25,833[b]
1954	276,120	80,670	26,737	78,100
1955	354,175	210,768[b]	35,545	215,248[b]
1956	380,611	261,454	27,408	251,175
1957	382,873	336,308	32,617	273,558
1958	490,340	179,437	73,100	111,357
1959	588,656	179,101	131,283	152,773
1960[c]	472,019	281,980	118,510	226,995

[a] The amounts for State Docks are included in the amounts for Wilmington.
[b] Discrepancy between the figures of the Corps of Engineers and those of the Authority.
[c] Additional tonnage: coastwise shipments, 4,200 tons; intercoastal receipts, 2,566 tons.
Source: For Wilmington, see source for Table 7; for State Docks, materials supplied by the State Ports Authority.

Port of Wilmington. The state terminal is thus fulfilling the purpose for which it was built. Shipments of domestic commerce are negligible at State Docks (see note c., Table 11). In addition to the important growth in general cargo at State Docks, there are increasing exports of wood pulp and scrap iron, and steel is expected to become an important item of export.

The following five tables (12-16) present tonnages of the individual commodities or groups of commodities moving through the two seaports and over the two state terminals. Several tables are necessary because statistics on the tonnages of individual products at the state terminals are not available for the years since 1955. Because Ocean Terminals handles all the general cargo at Morehead City Harbor, the figures in Table 13 will, however, indicate closely the tonnages of the particular commodities at Ocean Terminals. Moreover, most of the liquid cargo uses the facilities of Ocean Terminals.

This same situation does not prevail at State Docks, where, although it is the leading general cargo terminal, it does not handle all the general cargo at the Port of Wilmington. Neither is State Docks a factor in handling liquid cargo. A comparison of Table 14 with Tables 15 and 16 will show a larger number of items in the latter two. These items began moving through the port after State Docks was opened; hence their tonnages indicate approximately the tonnages of such items handled at State Docks.

Personnel of the Bureau of Customs who have been familiar with operations at both ports for a number of years estimate that at Wilmington, except for petroleum products, fertilizer materials, and molasses and sugar, State Docks has been handling 90 per cent of the import and export activity. If the total import and export tonnages for these three groups of products were subtracted from the total imports and exports for the Port of Wilmington, the result, according to the Bureau of Customs, would represent a fairly accurate estimate of the activities at State Docks. At Morehead City all import and export activity is at Ocean Terminals except for petroleum products.[3]

Table 12 presents the tonnages of deep-water commerce (foreign and coastwise) at Morehead City Harbor for 1952 and for Ocean Terminals for the following three years. The data for the three years supplied by the Authority do not distinguish between foreign

[3] James E. Townsend, Assistant Collector of Customs, Bureau of Customs, Wilmington, N. C., to author, Aug. 21, 1961.

and coastwise shipments, but class all movements under exports and imports. Glycol actually moves in coastwise shipments and a portion of the petroleum products are coastwise receipts. Some of the other products moved as domestic instead of foreign commerce.

Table 12. Tonnages of the Principal Items of Deep-Water Commerce at Ocean Terminals

Commodity	1952[a]	1953	1954	1955
Exports				
Fish oil	—	—	—	391
Glycol	—	3,231	6,229	11,002
Soy beans	—	—	—	826
Tobacco	—	3,131	3,879	4,475
Vehicles[b]	—	4,937	—	—
Military				
Vehicles and equipment	—	87,954	210,905	187,144
Imports				
Fertilizer	—	21,348	845	—
Petroleum	305,385	359,308	272,046	218,613
Asphalt and fuel oil	37,531	45,197	75,802	62,365
Sugar	—	—	1,456	1,499
Industrial Chemicals	23,658	—	—	—
Total	366,574	425,106	571,162	486,315

[a] For Morehead City Harbor.
[b] Military, sent in commercial ships.
Source: 1952, Report of Chief of Engineers, U. S. Army; 1953, 1954, 1955, materials supplied by the State Ports Authority.

Table 13 shows the items of deep-water commerce at Morehead City Harbor for the years 1956 through 1960. The number of items of foreign commerce has increased considerably since 1956. In that year there were 14 classes of exports and imports combined. For the succeeding four years the number was 21, 30, 30, and 30, respectively.

Table 14 presents the volume of the different exports and imports at State Docks for the four years, 1952 through 1955. The increase in the number of items and particularly in the tonnages handled is evident. Rather wide fluctuations are noticeable from year to year in some items.

As was stated previously, the tonnages of individual items at the state terminals are not available for the years since 1955, but such figures are obtainable for the entire port. Consequently, a rough idea of the tonnages of the different export and import items at State Docks may be gained by presenting these tonnages for the Port of Wilmington, which is done in Tables 15 and 16. Unlike Ocean Terminals,

Table 13. Tonnages of Deep-Water Commerce at Morehead City Harbor

Commodity	1956	1957	1958	1959	1960
Exports					
Tobacco, unmanufactured	9,767	14,384	25,697	35,312	36,241
Animal products, inedible	2,984	3,692	3,496	7,710	12,176
Animal feeds, grain, soybeans	15,338	—	11,183	22,005	21,226
Meat and products, fresh	30	14	41	87	99
Fruits and preparations, fresh	51	—	157	—	—
Logs	—	101	125	852	141
Lumber and other wood manufactures	16	102	846	1,505	3,092
Paper and manufactures	—	—	182	243	80
Vegetable and synthetic fibers and manufactures	—	66	5	1	9
Machinery and parts	20	—	4	170	118
Motor vehicles, except SCi[a]	1,643	—	—	—	—
Commodities nec,[b] except SCi	—	8,830	8,635	5,427	—
Miscellaneous items[c]	49	12	44	—	3,930
Total	29,898	27,201	50,415	73,312	77,112
Imports					
Motor fuel and fuel oil	30,841	98,201	89,647	86,244	133,348
Petroleum asphalt	56,872	61,341	64,112	70,613	78,357
Vegetables and preparations, fresh, canned	—	1,958	—	3,220	1,695
Steel mill products	—	—	340	754	129
Tools, basic hardware, metal manufactures and parts	—	8	282	625	770
Lumber and shingles	—	—	963	380	1,916
Vegetable fibers and manufactures	—	2	5	42	30
Fertilizer and materials	—	28	195	27	—
Miscellaneous items[d]	—	14	176	72	799
Total	87,713	161,552	155,720	161,977	217,044
Coastwise Shipments					
Industrial chemicals	13,400	15,379	9,477	11,788	20,189
Petroleum products	—	—	—	3,134	2,894
Soybeans	—	2,827	—	—	—
Total	13,400	18,206	9,477	14,922	23,158[e]
Coastwise Receipts					
Petroleum products	169,539	129,889	143,664	190,217	226,768
Industrial chemicals	40,445	—	—	—	—
Stone and manufactures	3,799	—	—	—	—
Total	213,783	129,889	143,664	190,217	226,768
Grand Total	344,784	336,848	359,276	440,428	544,082

[a] Special category items: shipments of non-Department of Defense military component items.

[b] "Nec" means not elsewhere classified.

[c] Includes crude drugs, herbs, and roots; fertilizer materials; dried milk; manganese; rolled steel products; industrial chemicals, nec; table beverages; and low-value shipments.

[d] Includes tobacco leaf; vegetable products, inedible; liquors and wines; vegetable oils; shellfish products; glass and glass products; vehicles and parts; and U. S. articles returned.

[e] Includes 75 tons of "commodities nec."

Source: Waterborne Commerce of the United States.

State Docks has only a negligible amount of coastwise commerce (see note c., Table 11) and therefore tonnages for that traffic are not given.

State Docks handles both bulk and general cargo. The items of bulk cargo may be identified in Table 14 and then be compared with the same items in Tables 15 and 16. The new items that have been added from year to year provide an approximation of the commodities comprising the general cargo.

Table 14. Tonnages of the Principal Exports and Imports at State Docks

Commodity	1952	1953	1954	1955
Exports				
Cottonseed meal and oil	—	11,678	—	2,394
Butter and butter oil	—	—	—	9,190
Cheese	—	—	—	5,068
Dried milk	—	1,541	2,653	11,693
Scrap metal	—	—	47,407	150,808
Tobacco leaf	—	11,871	13,638	18,698
Wood pulp	91	—	5,158	10,872
Military				
Vehicles and equipment	—	715	8,198	4,168
Imports				
Burlap	—	1,119	3,118	4,117
Jute and jute webbing	—	—	550	1,468
Cotton	—	—	212	434
Fertilizer	19,883	51,921	9,836	16,505
Hardware	—	714	3,605	—
Lumber	—	937	—	2,180
Mahogany	—	—	1,856	—
Rayon fiber	—	—	—	1,399
Steel products	1,157	164	2,682	10,214
Sugar, raw	—	5,779	—	—
Sugar, refined	—	9,306	—	—
Total	21,131	95,745	98,913	249,208

Source: Materials supplied by the State Ports Authority.

Table 15 gives the tonnages for the different import commodities or groups of commodities at the Port of Wilmington. Table 16 is a similar one for exports.

This chapter has presented a general outline of the volume and of the composition of the commerce at the two seaports of the state and at the two state terminals. The next chapter discusses the development of the principal items of traffic at the state terminals and comments briefly on many items of lesser importance. The problems met and the methods used in promoting the ports—in selling them to shippers and receivers of freight and in competing with neighboring seaports—are treated.

Table 15. Tonnages of the Different Import Items at the Port of Wilmington

Item	1956	1957	1958	1959	1960
Petroleum and products	156,030	169,641	185,326	235,176	156,159
Fertilizer materials	130,090	109,294	138,747	139,100	118,197
Sugar	26,644	30,596	26,813	22,084	22,473
Molasses, sugar products, edible	4,282	2,909	2,376	5,513	3,418
Molasses, inedible	25,430	20,807	29,310	25,968	25,708
Burlap and jute bagging	6,560	6,206	5,888	6,407	6,162
Coal-tar products	16,034	9,281	21,658	10,891	15,159
Rolled, finished steel mill products	9,348	8,790	11,371	39,071	27,643
Tools and basic hardware	3,981	4,868	7,096	13,669	14,846
Sulphur	—	12,430	17,138	17,189	19,934
Manganese	—	4,222	13,160	11,518	4,312
Cotton, unmanufactured	289	94	2,074	403	143
Cotton, manufactures	108	81	64	150	496
Synthetic fibers, manufactures	640	40	3,159	6,684	2,987
Vegetable fibers, manufactures nec	89	104	272	61	91
Wool, unmanufactured	—	—	—	462	33
Wool, manufactures	—	—	—	459	1,191
Textile products nec	20	234	147	172	264
Tea	—	119	80	183	96
Liquors and wines	20	236	268	343	519
Table beverage materials nec	18	17	15	37	20
Tobacco, unmanufactured	—	—	—	3,895	9,622
Vegetables and preparations, including canned	233	—	13	—	29
Fruits and preparations, fresh, canned	—	324	—	137	201
Vegetable products, inedible	25	19	17	249	276
Animals, products, inedible	27	5	—	814	395
Logs, posts, poles, and piling	—	—	120	913	3,031
Lumber, other manufactures of wood	6	3	7,941	20,792	16,975
Paper and manufactures	—	586	1,632	2,179	2,847
Textile, shoe machinery, parts	—	63	151	443	803
Other machinery, parts	53	243	738	1,519	1,392
Motor vehicles, parts	—	21	401	488	228
Iron and steel pipe	—	—	11,040	15,662	8,134
Metal manufactures, parts nec	60	126	321	822	424
Lead and alloys	—	78	222	261	520
Copper, semifabricated alloy, forms, scrap	115	77	437	518	539
Glass and glass products	328	133	194	563	463
Industrial chemicals	—	740	1,419	2,163	2,760
Commodities nec	71	52	37	138	324
Miscellaneous items[a]	89	67	212	875	29,133
U. S. articles returned	21	367	483	685	1,231
Total	380,611	382,873	490,340	588,656	472,019

[a] Includes: semimanufactured cotton; nuts and preparations; meat and meat products; spices; aircraft and watercraft, and parts; clay products, brick, and tile; tin metal forms; rubber manufactures; hides and skins; leather and leather manufactures; aluminum metals and alloys; semifinished iron and steel; ferrous castings, forgings; kitchen and hospital utensils; fish and products; hides and skins; vegetable dyeing and tanning materials; nonmetallic minerals, manufactures nec; precious metals and manufactures; pigments, paints, varnishes; and less than 2,000 pound shipments.

Source: Waterborne Commerce of the United States.

Table 16. Tonnages of the Different Export Items at the Port of Wilmington

Item	1956	1957	1958	1959	1960
Tobacco, unmanufactured	15,748	21,160	26,312	16,670	13,927
Iron and steel scrap	197,073	178,370	15,818	81,265	148,665
Wood pulp	15,511	37,008	33,082	38,675	59,008
Dried milk and solids, cheese	6,127	10,855	2,349	83	5,465
Animal feeds	7,377	5,169	1,759	764	292
Logs, posts, poles, and piling	308	110	—	323	246
Lumber, other manufactures of wood	91	1,197	2,585	1,166	899
Engines, turbines, parts	1	1,167	2,261	2,100	1,467
Textile, shoe machinery, parts	21	13	587	611	942
Other machinery, parts	133	257	517	120	128
Motor vehicles, parts, except SCi	710	4	2	31	38
Crude drugs, herbs, roots	21	24	38	13	8
Paper and manufactures	111	16	306	57	631
Aluminum ores, alloys, metals, concentrates, scrap	—	—	17	3,493	6,780
Metal manufactures, parts, nec, except SCi	—	18	20	85	15
Nonmetallic minerals, manufactures nec	—	111	573	76	—
Chemical specialties, except SCi	—	17	53	209	64
Phosphate fertilizer material	4,000	—	—	—	—
Cotton manufactures	—	19	18	184	915
Synthetic fibers, manufactures	—	28	567	465	760
Commodities nec, except SCi	4,042	15,564	18,882	9,751	11
Miscellaneous items[a]	69	146	197	728	533
Department of Defense and SCi	14,111	65,055	73,494	22,232	41,224
Total	265,454	336,308	179,437	179,101	281,980

[a] Includes: cotton, unmanufactured and semimanufactured; tools and basic hardware; industrial chemicals; ferroalloys, ores, and metals; leather and manufactures; glass and glass products; rubber manufactures; clays and earths; iron and steel pipe; textile products, nec; molasses, sugar products, edible; shells unmanufactured; inedible animal products; meat and products; vegetables and preparations; copper products; and $100-$499 valued shipments.

Source: Waterborne Commerce of the United States.

6. The Development of the Major Classes of Commerce at the State Terminals

An examination of Tables 12-16 in the preceding chapter will reveal that certain commodities and commodity groups supply the major part of the commercial tonnage at the state terminals. There are many other items, particularly at State Docks, which supply small annual tonnages or occasional tonnages. Not every individual product is identified in these tables. Some of them are included in a group with similar or allied products. For example, the following commodities have been handled at State Docks: bananas, beet pulp, carpets and rugs, cocoa powder and grounder shells, coconuts, glucose, fish meal, leather meal, matches, mica, peat moss, picture framing, telephone cable, unglazed doors, wooden doors, wild animals, cooperage materials, bonding mortar, and tankage.

Excluding liquid cargo, the leading tonnage items at Ocean Terminals are leaf tobacco, grains and soybeans, fish oil (called "inedible animal products" in the tables), and a group called "commodities nec" by the Corps of Engineers. All of these products are exports. Ocean Terminals has no important item of general cargo that is imported. One item of liquid cargo, namely asphalt, is discussed later because of its relationship to the promotion of certain other kinds of traffic.

At State Docks the major exports are scrap metal, wood pulp, leaf tobacco, machinery of various kinds, forest products and manufactures thereof, and commodities nec. The leading imports are burlap and jute bagging, finished steel mill products, tools and hardware, synthetic fibers and manufactures thereof, and lumber and other manufactures of wood.

Most of the remainder of this chapter is a discussion of the development of deep-water commerce in these more important commodities. Certain other attempts to promote traffic, some successful, some not, are mentioned briefly.

Tobacco

Earlier it was stated that the Authority planned to develop Morehead City as a tobacco-exporting point. This program has been so successful that the city has become one of the nation's leading tobacco-exporting centers. J. Harry White of Winston-Salem, a retired executive of a tobacco company and a member of the first three boards of the Authority, was one of those who took an active part in promoting the shipment of leaf tobacco through the state ports.

Morehead City handled its first cargo of tobacco in 1953, a shipment destined for Europe. In 1949 representatives of Universal Leaf Tobacco Company and the Export Leaf Tobacco Company, both of Richmond, informed the Authority that their firms would consider both Morehead City and Wilmington for exporting tobacco if those ports could compete with Norfolk and Charleston in economical storage and shipping charges, efficient service, and regular sailings. These firms stated they would require an aggregate storage space for 25,000 hogsheads of tobacco at each port.

To encourage shipments to Morehead City, the Atlantic and East Carolina Railroad, in the fall of 1952, submitted a proposal to the Southern Freight Association for adjusting rates on tobacco in hogsheads from the principal redrying points to Morehead City. The rates then in force were exception class rates which were much higher than rates to Hampton Roads ports and Wilmington. This proposal was turned down. The tobacco exporters moved cargoes to Morehead City in their own trucks. In March, 1953, the Common Carrier Tobacco Truck Lines were requested to adjust rates on tobacco into Morehead City with those in effect to Hampton Roads and Wilmington. The trucking firms filed such rates, which became effective in May, 1953. The Atlantic and East Carolina Railway then submitted another request to the Southern Freight Association which permitted rail rates from many, but not all, producing points to be adjusted to a competitive basis with truck rates as well as placing the port in a competitive position with Hampton Roads ports.[1]

The following data show comparative charges for an export rail

[1] *North Carolina Ports,* Jan., 1954, p. 15.

shipment of 38,000 pounds of tobacco leaf in hogsheads from various points of origin to competitive seaports after the preceding adjustments were made:[2]

| From | To | | | |
	Norfolk	Morehead City	Wilmington	Charleston
Fairmont	$148.20	$148.20	$ 76.40	$ 98.80
Goldsboro	99.40	82.20	82.20	148.20
Kinston	99.40	61.20	82.20	148.20
Washington	99.40	82.20	125.40	239.40
Lumberton	148.20	—	76.00	98.90
Greenville	99.40	82.20	82.20	231.80

Source: Materials of the State Ports Authority in the State Department of Archives and History, undated.

In 1953 about a score of tobacco leaf exporters in North Carolina indorsed a plan for expanded storage space at Morehead City and indicated readiness to commit definite amounts of tobacco for shipside warehousing. Most of these exporters suggested a storage capacity for 25,000 hogsheads, but some suggested 50,000 hogsheads. All but one of the firms felt that if space for 50,000 hogsheads were provided it should be at one port, and the majority favored Morehead City.[3] At the same time businessmen in Wilmington indicated they would support financing of additional storage space for tobacco.

The Authority had indorsed a program for the expansion of storage space at both ports in March, 1953. This decision was made after L. T. Weeks, the manager of the Five-State Flue-cured Tobacco Cooperative Association, said that this organization would need storage space for about 30,000 hogsheads of the 1953 crop. The initial movement of tobacco for this association was limited to 10,000 hogsheads by the Authority, and it moved from Wilmington in late 1953 and early 1954.[4] The Authority estimated that independent leaf exporters could utilize an added space for 12,000 hogsheads. Furthermore, the type of building required, although of cheaper construction than the main terminal buildings, would accommodate most types of dry cargo.

[2] This tabulation and similar ones later in this chapter do not give current freight rates or charges. Such data are presented for the purpose of showing rate relationships between competing ports. The relationships, however, may still prevail in spite of adjustments in rates or changes in the general level of rates.
[3] *Durham Morning Herald*, Sept. 15, 1953, 1:2.
[4] *North Carolina Ports*, Jan., 1954, p. 14.

On January 1, 1955, a Japanese ship arrived to take the first cargo of tobacco from Morehead City to Japan. At the same time another ship was loading tobacco for Germany. Another realized objective was the beginning of tobacco shipments to Holland in 1955. During the first quarter of 1955 five steamship cargoes of tobacco were loaded for export at Morehead City.[5] In late summer of 1955 the North German Lloyd's new *M. S. Baerenstein* of 5,547 gross tons made a one-day call at Morehead City, during which time it loaded 850,000 pounds of tobacco for shipment to Hamburg. The tobacco was supplied by a large dealer of eastern North Carolina and was consigned to one of Germany's large tobacco dealers.

A statement by a leading tobacco dealer summarizes the advantages of Morehead City as a point of export for tobacco:

By having tobacco shipped from redrying plants in my area of business, a great deal of time and money is saved, because of the shorter distance to Morehead City terminal as compared to the ports north of Morehead City. This short haul permits trucks to make, in many cases, two hauls per day, whereas a truck-load going to the next northern port usually requires a day and a half.[6]

Ships calling at Ocean Terminals for tobacco also pick up small quantities of several other commodities, among which are barrel staves, oranges, frozen poultry, fish oil, and deer tongue.[7] As more tobacco is offered for export more vessels will be attracted to the port, and the attraction of a wider range of other commodities can be expected.

Tobacco is also exported through the port at Wilmington. It has moved over the private docks for many years and State Docks has been handling increasing amounts. The Imperial Tobacco Company, Ltd., which supplied the first shipment of tobacco over State Docks, is an important exporter. During 1953 five different vessels loaded cargoes ranging from 2,100 to 5,000 hogsheads each for that company.[8] The leaf exported at the state ports is chiefly North Carolina flue-cured, but there is also some Kentucky burley.

[5] *Manufacturer's Record*, May, 1955, p. 60.

[6] L. B. Jenkins of Kinston, N. C., in *North Carolina State Ports*, Nov., 1954, p. 4.

[7] Deer tongue, a plant which grows wild in the Morehead City–Wilmington area, is the source of an essential oil (coumarin) with the odor of vanilla. This oil is highly regarded as a flavoring agent for tobacco in Europe, particularly by the Germans. The dried leaves are packed into bales of 450 pounds each for export (*North Carolina State Ports*, April, 1959, p. 15).

[8] *North Carolina Ports*, Dec., 1953, p. 22.

Table 17 shows the exports of tobacco leaf at the North Carolina seaports and their leading competitors. The outstanding feature is the simultaneous decline of Norfolk and rise of Morehead City. Charleston has also declined in importance, although it never ranked with Norfolk or Wilmington, while Wilmington has increased since the opening of State Docks in 1952. All the tonnage at Morehead City moves over Ocean Terminals.

It was pointed out in Chapter I (p. 12) that the Buckley Report stated there should be a division of leaf tobacco exports of 26 per cent for Morehead City and 74 per cent for Wilmington, on the basis of competitive conditions existing at the time the report was made. Table 17 shows Morehead City in a much more important position now.

Table 17. Tonnages of Exports of Unmanufactured Tobacco from Norfolk, Charleston, Wilmington, and Morehead City, 1946-1960

Year	Norfolk	Charleston	Wilmington	Morehead City
1946	140,001	—	44,312	—
1947	95,530	581	9,195	—
1948	78,476	10,523	21,660	—
1949	101,588	7,718	21,960	—
1950	111,964	8,267	11,126	—
1951	110,669	1,555	14,230	—
1952	62,540	2,675	3,180	—
1953	85,706	6,364	9,198	3,141
1954	68,483	1,405	13,638	4,066
1955	76,633	3,104	19,666	4,479
1956	77,619	2,429	15,748	9,767
1957	74,346	1,639	21,160	14,384
1958	56,073	1,052	26,312	25,697
1959	55,697	170	16,670	35,312
1960	79,222	231	13,927	36,241

Source: See source to Table 7.

Grain and Soybeans

The first shipment of grain from Ocean Terminals was made by barge to Baltimore in early 1955. Attempts by the Authority to develop the outward movement of grain and soybeans at Morehead City, at first unsuccessful, now seem to be starting to bear fruit. These products move for export and for coastwise and internal domestic shipments. For a volume movement, however, there must be favorable freight rates from the Midwest. With the entry of the Southern Railway into Morehead City such rates have now been realized. However, the movement of grain and soybeans is being built at present on the basis of the North Carolina production of these commodities, and this production has been increasing for several years.

The federal agricultural control program has brought about a decline in the acreages in some crops and has left the land available for growing other crops. Table 18 shows a decline in the average acreage harvested for the period 1942-1951 compared with the period 1952-1959, for cotton, tobacco, corn, and wheat, but a reduction in the average output only in cotton. Oats, sorghum for grains, and soybeans for beans, all had increases in both the average acreage harvested and the average production.

Table 18. Acreage Harvested and Production for Selected Crops During Selected Periods in North Carolina (in thousands)

Commodity	1942-1951[a]		1952-1960[b]	
	Acres	Production[c]	Acres	Production[c]
Cotton	719	522	498	366
Tobacco	680	790,858	593	879,616
Corn	2,232	61,059	2,032	68,132
Oats	354	10,206	431	15,273
Sorghum for grain	14	390	83	2,353
Wheat	427	6,860	367	8,057
Soybeans for beans	252	3,434	367	7,131

[a] 10-year average.
[b] 9-year average.
[c] Production is in bales for cotton, pounds for tobacco, and bushels for the remaining items.
Source: Agricultural Marketing Service, U. S. Department of Agriculture.

In order to attract these products the Authority built a grain-handling facility in 1955 at a cost of $80,000, financed with an issue of revenue bonds by the Authority. This facility was leased to Cargill, Inc., who moved grain in from the Midwest by rail. Government surplus oats from the Carolinas was moved in by truck and stored in a warehouse leased by Cargill, Inc., until it was sold abroad, when it would move on government contract. The first export shipment of bulk grain was made late in 1956 with the shipment of a cargo to Scandinavian countries for cattle feed.

Cargill, Inc., used this facility a year and then decided to build a large grain elevator in Norfolk. The Authority made an unsuccessful effort to have the firm build an elevator at either Morehead City or Wilmington.   The facility was idle from the end of 1956 until late in 1958, when it was put into operation by a new firm.

The grain-handling facility is now leased jointly by the Tar Heel Grain Company, Inc., of Speed, North Carolina, and Fred Webb, Inc., of Greenville, North Carolina.   The former firm is a wholly owned subsidiary of P. R. Markley, Inc., of Philadelphia, Pennsylvania. Fred Webb, Inc., has access to 2.5 million bushels of grain-storing facilities located in inland North Carolina at Greenville, Tarboro, and Washington.   The new company, called the Carolina Grain Company, assumed the remaining indebtedness.   Cargill, Inc., had paid nearly $69,000 in principal and interest in its one year of operation. The original lease with the new tenant expired on December 31, 1959, with an option to renew it for five years.   After December 31, 1959, the new firm agreed to pay an annual rental and to ship a substantial amount of tonnage each year.   The terms of the agreement assure payment of the outstanding bonds issued to construct the facility and provide sufficient funds to pay the lease cancellation requirements and meet all expenses connected with the purchase of grain-handling equipment from Cargill, Inc., which that company had installed.   The Authority derives revenue through grain-handling charges.

In 1958 special facilities which will unload as much as 350 tons of grain and soybeans an hour were installed.   These facilities were put into operation late in 1958 to load a shipload of 7,000 tons of corn, most of which was destined for the Netherlands and Germany.

The Carolina Grain Company now has five tanks with a storage capacity of 110,000 bushels located on property of the Authority and a warehouse with a storage capacity of 75,000 bushels.   Official weighing and inspection is done by the North Carolina Department of Agriculture.

When the grain elevator was built in 1955, the Authority hoped it would be managed in a manner that would develop an important grain trade for the port.   Apparently, Cargill, Inc., was interested primarily in the year-to-year advantages it could realize from the undertaking.   To some extent the two objectives were contradictory.

The possibilities for success seem to be greater under the arrangement with the Carolina Grain Company.   Local people who are interested in the economic development of the region on which they rely primarily for their incomes are associated with this company.

Hence, the grain trade will be built largely on the basis of the production of these commodities in the trade territory of Morehead City. Local interests are more likely to do whatever is required to stimulate this production than is an outside firm like Cargill, Inc.

Thus far there have been only occasional cargoes of grain and allied products. In 1955, 1,890 tons of soybeans were shipped in internal commerce. In 1957, 2,945 tons of soybeans were received in internal commerce, and 2,827 tons were shipped in coastwise commerce. In 1957, 5,921 tons of oats were shipped in internal commerce. In 1956 there were 15,338 tons of foreign exports of "animal feeds, nec.," and in 1958 there were 11,183 tons of corn exports. In 1960 there were 15,714 tons of wheat and 5,512 tons of soybeans exported, while 597 tons of wheat and 2,171 tons of soybeans were moved in internal shipments.

Fish Oil

In early 1955 the export of the first tanker of fish oil was made from Ocean Terminals. This oil, the product of the menhaden fishing industry, was destined for Germany, where it is used in the manufacture of oleomargarine. Formerly the oil had moved to New York City for transshipment.[9] The second shipment of fish oil to move through Ocean Terminals was loaded in January, 1956. More than 700 tons were poured into the storage tanks of the *M. V. Goetlingen* calling on her maiden voyage. More than 700,000 pounds of leaf tobacco also were loaded on the ship.

The menhaden has been providing oil, animal feed, and fertilizer since colonial times. A large portion of its body becomes fish meal, an important ingredient of poultry feed. New uses have been developed for menhaden oil lately, including hot dip tinning, terne plating and galvanizing, the manufacture of insulating varnishes, ship bottom paints, soaps, rubber products, and others.[10] Morehead City, Beaufort, Wilmington, and Southport are the principal processing centers in the state for menhaden, and Ocean Terminals is the major export point for fish oil. Menhaden oil arrives at port by truck in specially made containers. The oil is pumped from the

[9] *Ibid.,* Feb., 1955, p. 18.
[10] *Ibid.,* Nov., 1959, pp. 4-5.

container to a tank and from the tank to waiting tank ships for shipment to foreign markets.

Separate statistics on the exports of fish oil are not available.   In *Waterborne Commerce of the United States,* fish oil is included with "animal products, inedible," the exports of which are found in Table 13 of the preceding chapter.

Forest Products

The development of commerce in logs and lumber, particularly at State Docks, has been one of the objectives of the Authority.   The facilities for handling lumber have been expanded recently at both ports.   In 1960 a new warehouse for operation by a European Company, the Continental Lumber Company (also called Continental Timbers, Inc., in *Ties,* December, 1960, p. 11), was constructed and leased to the company.   This firm is engaged in exporting North Carolina logs and lumber to western Europe[11] and uses the warehouse for accumulating cargoes of these products.

W. Avery Thompson and J. E. Thompson, both lumber dealers of southeastern North Carolina, and Harold F. Coffey, a furniture manufacturer of Lenoir, all of whom were members of the Authority at the time, took leading parts in promoting commerce in logs and lumber at the state terminals.   In December, 1953, the first waterborne movement of Canadian fir lumber arrived after more than a year's effort to provide steamship space for Canadian lumber from the Pacific Northwest.   There was also a demand in the port area for California redwood and other Pacific coast lumber which came in by railroad.   Intercoastal ships were unable to offer space for South Atlantic ports in many instances.   These ships earn greater revenues to points north of Cape Hatteras than to points south of it and therefore fill out the cargoes with shipments to the more northern ports.   A solution is to be found in foreign flagships from Canadian ports, the fir mentioned having moved previously in a Panamanian ship, but this method is not a solution for transporting from West Coast ports.[12]

Mahogany, from both the Philippines and Central America, is

[11] Bruce, *op. cit.*
[12] *North Carolina Ports,* Dec., 1953, p. 12.

another wood in heavy demand in the hinterlands of the seaports of North Carolina. This wood has several uses, the most important of which are for veneer in the furniture industry and for plywood. North Carolina is the leading state in the manufacture of wooden furniture and of hardwood plywood, the two industries which utilize most of the tropical hardwood imports. At present most of the tropical wood veneers used in North Carolina are from midwestern plants, with small amounts from plants at Norfolk and New Orleans, and the tropical woods that are processed in North Carolina usually have been imported through Norfolk and Charleston. Small shipments of mahogany, however, have begun arriving at State Docks in Wilmington, and a competent authority believes it would be logical to process tropical woods into veneer and plywood at both Wilmington and Morehead City.[13] If processing plants were located in these cities, important savings in transportation charges would result, which would strengthen the competitive position of the industries of the state which use tropical hardwoods as a material in their products. One dealer in mahogany who has started to import through Wilmington has said, "Because of efficient handling and unloading of my mahogany from the Philippines at the North Carolina State Port, I realize not only a saving to myself but also to the furniture industry and all those connected with us in using our stock."[14]

The following tabulation shows comparative rail charges on 34,000 pounds of mahogany lumber from the different competing ports to several destinations:

	From			
To	Norfolk	Morehead City	Wilmington	Charleston
Asheboro	$156.40	$163.20	$142.80	$146.20
Goldsboro	132.60	125.80	125.80	163.20
Greensboro	170.00	190.40	139.40	176.80
Sanford	146.20	142.80	125.80	146.20

Source: Files of the State Ports Authority in the State Department of Archives and History, undated.

Mahogany lumber from Central America is brought directly to State Docks by a New Orleans firm which specializes in the manu-

[13] See James S. Bethel, "Opportunities for Processing Tropical Woods in North Carolina," *Resource Industry Series No. 7*, North Carolina Department of Conservation and Development and North Carolina State Ports Authority. Mimeographed, 1951, pp. 1, 2, 7, 8.
[14] *North Carolina State Ports*, Nov., 1954, p. 2.

facture, importing, and exporting of mahogany and veneer. A portion of the shipments is placed in storage yards at State Docks.

Other forest species which move through State Docks are obeche, greenheart, virola, and pine logs. The initial shipment of obeche logs arrived in November, 1959. Veneer for interior construction is made from this species, in which it supplements domestic gum and poplar. Obeche has been used for many years by plywood manufacturers in Europe and England. Destination points in the United States are more easily served by Wilmington than by other South Atlantic ports.[15] Greenheart logs are imported from South America. This species is resistant to marine borers, fire, and abrasion. It is used for piers, railway trestles, bridges, and heavy-duty flooring. Virola is a wood from South America used as a core for veneer furniture. Pine logs are exported from Wilmington to the Netherlands and railroad crossties to Western Europe.

Table 19 shows the predominance of Norfolk, compared with Wilmington and Charleston, in importing logs. For Norfolk, though, the figures indicate a declining trend. Other influences than competition among the ports account for this trend.

Table 19. Tonnages of Foreign Imports of Logs at Wilmington, Norfolk, and Charleston, 1947-1951 and 1952-1960

Year	Wilmington	Norfolk	Charleston
1947-51	2,287[a]	46,728[b]	24,188[c]
1952	—	22,374	1,894
1953	—	41,390	—
1954	—	25,733	9
1955	—	28,051	13
1956	—	42,117	579
1957	—	18,890	—
1958	120	18,544	—
1959	678	21,037	39
1960	3,031	24,198	1,078

[a] For one year, 1948.
[b] 5-year average.
[c] 4-year average, 1948-1951.
Source: See source to Table 7.

Wood pulp recently established itself as one of the leading exports at State Docks. Its source is the plant of the Riegel Paper Corporation located at Acme, twenty miles inland from Wilmington. Nearness to ocean transportation was a strong influence in locating this plant. Shipments have gone to numerous countries in all parts of the

[15] *Ibid.*, Winter, 1960, p. 15.

world, where the pulp is combined with other pulps to make a variety of products. The company maintains a replanting program which should insure a permanent and growing item of export.

Attempts have been made to encourage the importation of newsprint through Morehead City, but buyers have expressed doubt as to the rail services there compared with those from Norfolk where most water shipments for North Carolina newspapers enter. Not all newsprint for use in North Carolina is shipped by water, but a substantial quantity moves through Norfolk and would supply considerable tonnage for the state ports if they could attract it. The total amount of newsprint used in the state is large. For example, in 1952 the Raleigh *News and Observer* used about 200 cars.[16]

Table 20 has rail rates on newsprint in 1952 from Norfolk and the North Carolina ports to a number of destinations. In no instance does Morehead City have a higher rate than Norfolk, and in a few cases it has a lower rate. In half of the cases Wilmington has a lower rate than Norfolk, and in no case is Wilmington's rate higher. Other factors than rates would account for the importance of Norfolk.

Table 20. Rail Rates on Newsprint to Selected Destinations from Competing Ports (in cents per cwt., 40,000 pounds minimum shipment)

To	From		
	Norfolk	Wilmington	Morehead City
Asheville	47	45	47
Charlotte	39	36	39
Durham	33	33	33
Goldsboro	28	25	25
Greensboro	36	36	36
High Point	37	37	37
Kinston	28	28	21
New Bern	31	25	17
Raleigh	32	30	32
Rocky Mount	—	29	29
Salisbury	38	37	38
Winston-Salem	38	38	38

Source: Letter of February 22, 1952, by E. R. Buchan, President, Atlantic & East Carolina Railway Company to H. G. Braxton, President, Kinston *Daily Free Press,* Kinston, N. C.

[16] Frank A. Daniels, general manager, *News and Observer,* to Col. George W. Gillette, executive director, State Ports Authority, Nov. 6, 1952. This letter is in the files of the State Ports Authority in the State Department of Archives and History.

Steel Products, Hardware, Machinery, and Vehicles

Another group of imports at Wilmington includes steel products and hardware items. A new firm, the Coastal Steel and Iron Company, has constructed a fabricating plant specializing in structural steel near Wilmington. A major portion of the steel will be from domestic sources, but there will also be foreign imports. The firm will use the Intracoastal Waterway for distributing some of its output.[17]

Another firm, the Woodward W. Williams Company of Columbia, South Carolina, has established a new distributing organization for steel products, known as the Steel Products Supply Company, with headquarters at State Docks. Its first imports were sizable amounts of wire products. Other steel products have been added to the firm's inventory as markets for them have developed.[18]

The American Hardware and Equipment Company, a wholesale hardware firm of Charlotte, North Carolina, imports numerous kinds of manufactured steel products from Europe. Included in the list are barbed wire, nails, fence posts, hinges, bicycles, and other products. These items are distributed by truck and railway in North Carolina, Tennessee, Kentucky, and Virginia. This firm is the exclusive distributor in the Carolinas for the European lightweight "Torpedo" bicycle. The president of the company said recently that it now imports goods exclusively through North Carolina ports and that the savings in time and money, compared with shipping overland from other Eastern ports such as Norfolk and New York, have made possible a greatly expanded import business for the firm. The wire and nails were produced under contract by four firms, this arrangement being the result of a purchasing trip to Europe in the spring of 1954 by the president of the American Hardware and Equipment Company who plans to explore the possibility of importing still other hardware items. This firm uses the State Docks at Wilmington because of their efficient handling of its products.[19]

Imports of agricultural hardware items are increasing through the State Docks at Wilmington because of (1) the economy resulting from scheduled sailings from Europe, (2) shorter traveling distances within the areas of the ports for distribution, and the savings resulting from deep-water transportation.[20]

[17] *North Carolina Ports*, Jan., 1954, p. 16.
[18] *Ibid.*
[19] For more details, see *ibid.*, Feb., 1955, p. 17.
[20] See *Manufacturer's Record*, March, 1955, p. 40.

The Farmers' Cooperative Exchange (FCX), which distributes products throughout the Carolinas, makes considerable use of the state ports, principally for importing steel products. The ports are excellent distribution points because the imported products are placed in close proximity to the final distribution point. The following tabulation of motor carrier charges on a shipment of 36,000 pounds of imported iron and steel articles indicates the rate relationships on these items between the different competing ports:

| To | From | | | |
	Norfolk	Morehead City	Wilmington	Charleston
High Point	$259.20	$244.80	$118.80	$147.60
Winston-Salem	259.20	259.20	129.60	147.60
Durham	219.60	208.80	104.40	147.60
Lumberton	259.20	219.60	68.40	111.60

Source: State Ports Authority files in the State Department of Archives and History, undated.

Occasional shipments of some steel products move through the state ports. For example, at Wilmington in late 1958 two ships unloaded 4,000 tons of steel pipe for a transmission line being constructed by the Natural Gas Corporation. One vessel was from England, the other from Germany.[21] Again, the German pump manufacturing firm of F. W. Pleuger opened a plant at Statesville at the end of 1960. Initially, parts for assembling the pumps will be shipped through Wilmington from the main plant in Hamburg, supplemented by parts from the Statesville plant.[22] A similar example involving machinery was the shipment of an entire rock-crushing plant to Nicaragua in 1959 from Ocean Terminals by the Nello L. Teer Construction Company of Durham, North Carolina.

Scrap iron and steel is an export item in this field. Special facilities for handling this item have been constructed at State Docks. Volume varies at both terminals, depending upon the state of prosperity in the nation's steel industry.

During the latter half of 1955 the first export of textile machinery through Wilmington was made. The machinery was manufactured in Charlotte and was destined for the Netherlands, where a firm was building the first cotton mill in Europe that would be completely

[21] *North Carolina State Ports,* Jan., 1959, p. 6.
[22] *Ibid.,* March, 1961, p. 14. The interest of this firm was aroused by a booklet published by the North Carolina Industry and Trade Commission to Europe.

equipped with American machinery.[23] In the same year a cargo of 400 tons of boiler components from the plant of the Babcock and Wilcox Marine Boiler Company was shipped to Spain for use in constructing a large power plant. In October, 1960, this firm exported four shiploads of boiler components for installations in both hemispheres. The shipment was one of the largest ever made at a North Carolina port.[24] Babcock and Wilcox selected Wilmington as the site for a plant because of State Docks. This company has assembly and storage facilities on the property of State Docks, from which it sends export shipments regularly.

Another recently developed item of traffic is the shipment of busses made for the federal government by the Perley A. Thomas Car Works at High Point. (The chassis of the bus is made in Detroit and the body is fitted to it in High Point.) The busses were being driven to either Norfolk or Charleston for shipment abroad. The cost to the government of getting a bus to Norfolk and Charleston was approximately $86.00 and $116.00, respectively. The cost to Wilmington was $73.00. Officials of the firm learned that the government maintains a list of port capabilities to be able to determine whether or not an item can be handled at a certain port. The firm enlightened the proper federal officials about the state terminals, and both were added to the list. The government then gave consideration to Wilmington as a possible port of exit for other shipments. By early 1961 more than a hundred busses had been shipped through the state ports, chiefly at Wilmington. Other cargoes go along with the busses. Added ships come to pick up these shipments.

Fibers and Textiles

Another group of commodities imported at Wilmington includes jute, burlap, and other jute products which are used for bagging by fertilizer, cottonseed oil, peanut, and potato producers, by seed and feed companies, and, in the form of piece goods, for wrapping and other uses by the furniture and textile industries. The representative of a firm which imports large cargoes of burlap and webbing said, "The two main reasons I bring my goods through the State Port are that

[23] *North Carolina State Ports,* Sept., 1955, p. 9.
[28] Bruce, *op. cit.*

I have saved my company time and money and that this saving can be passed along to our customers."[25]   This plant now imports about 20 million yards of burlap a year.   Its trade area is in the Carolinas, Virginia, and Georgia.

The handling of imported cotton is another activity which the Authority is trying to develop at State Docks. Textile manufacturers, brokers, and buyers are co-operating with the Authority in its attempts at attracting cotton shipments to the State Docks.   The fumigation plant mentioned previously aids in this respect.   The first cargoes of long-staple Egyptian cotton arrived at Wilmington in 1954.   This type of cotton has been imported mainly through Charleston for some time because that port built a fumigation plant in 1941 in order to attract this product.   Prior to that, Egyptian cotton had been imported at Boston.

Table 21 shows the imports of foreign cotton at Wilmington and Charleston since the state ports began operations. Thus far, Wilmington has not made any inroad on the business.   The cotton moves through Charleston because Wilmington does not have adequate storage facilities.

Table 21. Tonnages of Imports of Foreign Cotton at Wilmington and Charleston, 1952-1960

Year	Wilmington	Charleston
1952	—	18,845
1953	—	18,208
1954	212	15,622
1955	406	18,092
1956	289	10,794
1957	94	13,606
1958	2,074	17,295
1959	403	20,081
1960	143	30,977

Source: Waterborne Commerce of the United States.

In 1958 a 5,000-bale shipment of cotton which otherwise would have gone to Charleston was brought to Wilmington when there was not enough space at Charleston to handle it.   The result was so chaotic that no more cotton has been brought through State Docks.

The proximity of the state terminals to the textile distributing and manufacturing centers in North Carolina and bordering states is of particular importance in view of the keen competition in cotton

[25] North Carolina State Ports, Nov., 1954, p. 2.

textile manufacture. In an official announcement to the cotton trade, the Isthmian Steamship Company advertised that "as a service to the cotton industry we are offering in addition to our regular scheduled service from Alexandria, Egypt a direct call at Wilmington, North Carolina."[26] Wilmington is the first port of call this company makes upon the arrival of ships from India and Egypt. Thus cotton can be shipped inland earlier than if it went on to Charleston and one or more days of marine insurance is saved because of the earlier discharge.

The Authority has made an attempt to develop commerce at State Docks in cotton manufactures which move from the Piedmont in both export and coastwise trade. A comparison of Tables 16 and 23 indicates that the effort has not yet been successful. Until late in 1956 truck rates on cotton products discriminated in favor of Charleston. Volume truck rates to Norfolk and the North Carolina ports did not exist. Rail rates did not discriminate, but that mattered very little because the rail rates were the higher and most of the cotton textiles moving to a port went by truck. The cotton textile industry was almost exclusively in the Charleston trade territory.

In October, 1956, because of action by the Authority, volume rates by truck on cotton manufactures were published applicable to Norfolk and Wilmington but not to Morehead City. This action enlarged the territory of Wilmington, but Charleston still had an

[26] *Ibid.*, p. 3.

Table 22. Typical Motor Carrier Commodity Rates on Cotton Piece Goods and Related Products From Selected Points to Competing Ports (in cents per cwt.)

From	To		
	Charleston	Norfolk	Wilmington
Asheville	48	58	51
Burlington	40	39	39
Charlotte	40	50	38
High Point	40	43	39
Kannapolis	40	46	40
Newton	40	50	42
Raleigh	40	37	32
Roxboro	40	38	38
Troy	38	47	38
Winston-Salem	38	43	39

Source: Buckley Report, p. 158.

advantage at some North Carolina points.[27]   Table 22 gives the new rates from selected points in North Carolina to the competing ports. Minimum weights were 20,000 pounds for Charleston and Norfolk and 25,000 pounds for Wilmington.   Of the ten points, Charleston either had an advantage over or was equalized with Wilmington at five.

Table 23 shows shipments of manufacturers and semimanufacturers of cotton in the export and coastwise trades.   Such shipments for Wilmington are unimportant in quantity and are given in a footnote to the table.

Table 23. Tonnages of Foreign Exports and Coastwise Shipments of Manufactures and Semimanufactures of Cotton from Charleston and Norfolk

| | Charleston Harbor | | | | Norfolk Harbor | | | |
| | Manufactured | | Semimanufactured | | Manufactured | | Semimanufactured | |
Year	Exports	Coastwise	Exports	Coastwise	Exports	Coastwise	Exports	Coastwise
1946-51	10,236	1,810	10,567[a]	181[b]	2,643	1,879[c]	8,386[a]	—
1952	14,976	3,498	14,645	156	1,037	1,105	21,273	—
1953	13,602	3,375	25,379	15	2,274	2,072	15,526	—
1954	21,866	5,488	15,836	199	495	—	21,410	—
1955	19,825	500	12,605	76	557	3,735	25,818	15
1956	15,373	770	14,024	60	1,219	4,160	27,399	61
1957	19,428	1,266	25,620	243	3,144	3,039	19,916	153
1958	16,912	1,431	25,315	69	2,602	4,825	13,146	45
1959	15,491	2,604	26,036	154	2,004	2,363	20,652	27
1960	15,705	1,238	33,844	15	2,367	3,079	21,432	1

[a] 4-year average, 1948-51.
[b] 3-year average, 1949-51.
[c] For 1951.
Wilmington: No coastwise shipments.
    1948—exports, 11 tons manufactured, 3 tons semimanufactured.
    1957—exports, 19 tons manufactured, 20 tons semimanufactured.
    1958—exports, 18 tons manufactured.
    1959—exports, 184 tons manufactured.

The Buckley Report states that cotton textiles and textile products comprise a fertile field for the development of traffic for the state ports. These products are important from the standpoint of value per unit, and hence of high ocean freight rates, rather than tonnage.   The high freight rates are an attraction for ocean carriers to call at the ports.

Early in 1959, the first shipment of wool from Australia, a cargo of 2,880 bales, arrived at State Docks, where it was loaded into railway cars for destinations in the Carolinas and Virginia.   Much of the shipment was for plants of Burlington Industries, Inc.   With the gradual growth of the manufacture of woolen products in the Piedmont area, wool should be a growing import item.

[27] Buckley Report, p. 140.

A Goldsboro firm which manufactures chamois from sheepskins imported from New Zealand brings its raw material into the country through the state terminals. The greater share of the finished product is sold within the country, but some is exported through the state ports.

Asphalt

Asphalt is brought in by tanker from the Caribbean to Morehead City for the Trumbull Asphalt Company, the Fry Roofing Company, and the State Highway Commission. The asphalt is pumped several hundred yards through steam-insulated underground lines to the storage tanks of the buyers by the facilities of Ocean Terminals. During 1960 sixteen tankers brought in nineteen million gallons.

The Trumbull Asphalt Company packages asphalt in quarts, gallons, and five-gallon drums for the Sherwin-Williams Paint Company. The Fry Roofing Company, a next-door neighbor of Trumbull, which hauls roofing material that it manufactures into the hinterland, also distributes the packaged asphalt on the same trucks to Sherwin-Williams paint stores throughout the Carolinas, Virginia, and eastern Tennessee. Truck-trailers of the roofing company return to Morehead City loaded with grain being exported by the Carolina Grain Company.[28]

The Fry Roofing Company also brings in granules from Vermont by water and exports some of its finished product through Ocean Terminals. The advantages of water transportation influenced the location of this enterprise at Morehead City.

Earlier, a manufacturer of roofing material had located at Morehead City expecting to develop an export trade. The president of the company believed that this could be done if the city had the proper type of port. At the time this firm obtained asphalt from either Baltimore or Charleston at a rail rate of $7.80 a ton. If Morehead City had possessed the proper facilities for unloading asphalt, it could have been transported to Morehead City by barge for $2.00 a ton. As it was, owing to the cost advantages of roofing material manufactures at other ports, this firm could not compete in export markets.[29]

[28]Bruce, op. cit.
[29] C. C. Brewer, president, Madix Asphalt Roofing Company, Morehead City, to Col. George W. Gillette, executive director of the State Ports Authority, Nov. 2, 1948.

Government Surplus (CCC) Commodities

The Authority has been aware of the importance of movements of government surplus commodities in promoting traffic for the state terminals and has spent a considerable amount of effort in trying to obtain a share of this traffic. Grain and tobacco already have been mentioned in this connection. Other items are dairy products and cottonseed meal.

Numerous shipments of powdered milk have been made from State Docks. The first, in 1953, was a cargo of 2,800,000 pounds shipped by the United Nations to India for use in feeding undernourished children in the Far East. It was sent on a ship that had brought in burlap. In June, 1957, 3,000,000 pounds of surplus cheese was shipped from Morehead City to Yugoslavia under the CARE program. Cottonseed meal goes to Europe and is purchased from the Production and Marketing Administration of the United States Department of Agriculture. These surplus commodities move to the ports by rail from storage points, some from as far away as Wisconsin.

Transactions in surplus commodities are controlled by the provisions of Public Law 480. Surplus commodities are classified in three groups: (1) those sold at government cost, (2) those sold below cost, and (3) those given away under relief programs. For groups two and three, officials of the United States Department of Agriculture must police shipments to see if the price paid, freight rates, both land and ocean, and port charges are kept at the absolute minimum. Large amounts of these goods have moved through South Atlantic ports because of their greater economy. In group one above the government officials check the price paid and ocean freight rates, but not inland freight rates and other charges. None of this group has moved through South Atlantic ports. The Authority has tried to have the law modified so the state terminals can attract products in this group.[30]

Although these surplus commodities may move in large consignments, the annual volume may fluctuate widely from year to year (see Table 16). They are thus not as dependable revenue producers as some other products.

In the files of the States Ports Authority at the State Department of Archives and History.
[30] *North Carolina State Ports,* Fall, 1958, p. 17.

Other Products

At one time a distributor in Greenville, North Carolina, hoped to develop the importation of sugar at Morehead City, believing the port was "a natural point for Eastern North Carolina's supply."[81] Plans were made to import about 300,000 bags annually when the required terminal facilities were available. The storage and handling of refined sugar requires clean, fireproof facilities where the bats can be turned and "paddled" to prevent hardening. The first cargo was landed early in 1954. This commerce in sugar failed to develop. In only two years, namely, 1954 and 1955, have there been any sugar imports at Ocean Terminals. On the other hand, sugar has been an important import at the port of Wilmington for some time, and both raw and refined sugar from the Caribbean have moved through State Docks.

The importing of fertilizer and fertilizer materials was another activity which Ocean Terminals hoped to develop but which was unsuccessful. In 1952 and 1953 shipments of bulk fertilizer came in from Western Europe, but then the traffic was stopped because the fertilizer materials damaged the storage facilities. For the past few years small shipments have passed over Ocean Terminals. For many years materials for the manufacture of fertilizer have been a major import at the port of Wilmington, and since State Docks began operations many ships calling there have unloaded cargoes of these materials.

The Ideal Cement Company of Denver, Colorado, recently selected Wilmington as the site for a plant with an annual capacity of 1.5 million barrels. This cement plant is the first one to be built in the state. Marl, which will be mined in Pender and adjoining counties, will be the raw material. The company will have a distributing facility at Fayetteville, where a portion of its output will be transported by barge, and it has its own ships for hauling cement by ocean. This company should find a growing market for its product throughout the southeastern states. A portion of the output should move by coastwise trade.

In November, 1961, the Authority leased land at State Docks to the Diamond Alkali Company on which a $500,000 bulk caustic soda

[81] *North Carolina Ports*, Feb.-March, 1954, p. 14.

terminal was built.   This terminal, completed in 1962, supplies
caustic soda for the textile, paper and pulp, food processing, chemical,
and other industries in the area by rail, truck, and barge.

Large quantities of riprap (stones of irregular size), used for
making foundations or sea walls, move through the state terminals.
The stone is moved to barges and towed on the Intrascoastal Waterway
and across sounds to sites where it is used.

Seed potatoes from Prince Edward Island, Canada, are imported
annually at Morehead City.   The movement of potatoes into North
Carolina by boat was active during the 1930's, but the traffic declined
during the war.   In January, 1954, 10,000 bags of seed potatoes were
imported.   At present, about 65,000 bags are imported annually.[32]
Previously, the potatoes had been hauled overland from Norfolk
and other distant ports.   The direct shipment reduces loss because
there is less hauling and handling of the potatoes, which are stored
at Ocean Terminals to await final delivery to the farmers.   Ocean
Terminals is within easy reach of the potato growers, many of whom
haul the potatoes from the warehouse themselves.

Recently there have been small export shipments of frozen poultry.
This trade, if developed, might become important, because North
Carolina is one of the nation's leading states in the production of
broilers.

Several shipments of wild animals and one shipment of domestic
animals have been received at State Docks.   The wild animals included monkeys for phamaceutical companies and various other kinds
of tropical animals for circuses and zoos.   The cargo of domestic
animals was Arabian horses destined for a ranch in the southwestern
United States.

Passenger Traffic

In the fall of 1954 the Swedish steamer *M. S. Stockholm* was
taken off the Atlantic schedules and placed on schedules to Bermuda
and the Caribbean.   The Allen Travel Service of New York City ran
a series of vacation cruises which departed from Ocean Terminals.
The first cruise left on October 17 for Nassau and Cuba.   The majority of the four hundred passengers aboard were members of the

[32] *North Carolina State Ports,* April, 1959, p. 10.

North Carolina Academy of General Practice, which held its annual meeting aboard the vessel. There were also passengers from fifteen other states. Three other cruises followed, and the four cruises had a total of more than sixteen hundred passengers from thirty-two states.

During the fall of 1955 the Allen Travel Service conducted four cruises and chose Wilmington as the port of embarkation. This was the first time in thirty years that a cruise ship had left Wilmington. For the first one of these cruises, a voyage to Bermuda known as the "Governor's Cruise," Governor Luther H. Hodges and Mrs. Hodges made reservations. The North Carolina Automotive Wholesalers' Association booked passage on the same ship (the *Stockholm*) for its membership in order to hold its seasonal convention aboard, with the Governor giving the principal address.[33] Several other conventions of North Carolina business and professional groups have been held aboard ship on such cruises.

These trips have been continued up to the present time. In the fall of 1957 the Swedish-American Lines made three cruises from Wilmington to the Caribbean; all of them were sellouts. After the last trip the Allen Travel Service announced three scheduled sailings for the fall of 1958. In the winter and spring of 1958 the Arosa Lines made Wilmington a port of call on two cruises to the Caribbean and South America. These cruises were under the direction of the Caribbean Cruise Lines of Washington, D. C. The passengers have been enthusiastic about these trips. Good food, entertainment, and services are provided, and there are opportunities to shop at the ports where stops are made. Each cruise attracts up to four hundred passengers.[34] Table 24 shows the number of passengers sailing annually from each of the state terminals. The figures include military personnel.

State Docks needs a small passenger terminal to handle the passengers on these trips. At present, makeshift arrangements are employed. In March, 1960, the Authority adopted a new policy in regard to cruise ships operating out of the state ports. In the future these vessels will be given berth reservations in advance. Previously, berthing space had been assigned on a first-come, first-served basis.[35]

Passenger service also is available on freighters out of Morehead City. The Ozean-Stinnes Line has room for a maximum of twelve

[33] *Ibid.*, Winter, 1956, p. 14.
[34] For more details about the early cruises, see *ibid.*, Nov., 1954, p. 6; Feb., 1955, p. 18; Sept., 1955, p. 6.
[35] *Ibid.*, Spring, 1960, p. 11.

persons with a charge of $400 for a round trip to Western Europe. The ships return to State Docks every two weeks.[36]

The following chapter discusses the revenues, costs, and net profits associated with handling the commerce that has been described in the preceding two chapters. The costs are operating costs and do not cover interest on the state's investment in the ports nor anything for amortizing this investment. Neither are the annual appropriations by the state included when determining costs and net profits.

[36] *Ibid.*, July, 1959, p. 15.

Table 24. Passengers at Morehead City Harbor and the Port of Wilmington

Year	Morehead City	Wilmington
1946-51	3,345[a]	95[b]
1952	3,002	34
1953	6,000	67
1954	6,200	192
1955	5,610	1,171
1956	6,304	886
1957	12,025	11,727
1958	10,961	3,502
1959	30,511	5,565
1960	28,800	960

[a] 6-year average.
[b] 2-year average, 1950-51.
Source: See source to Table 7.

7. Expenses and Revenues

This chapter presents financial data relating to the administration and the operation of the two state terminals. Prior to the middle of 1952, activities were associated with construction and promotion. Since then both kinds have continued and, in addition, there have been those activities associated with operating the ports. The statistical data which follow cover the different classes and items of expense, including depreciation and sources of revenue.

Expenditures

As has been stated previously, the Authority receives funds from two different sources, namely, state appropriations and port operations, and the spending of the funds from each source must be accounted for separately. There are therefore two broad classes of expenses. First are those expenses arising out of the functioning of the Authority itself, and second are those resulting from the operations of the ports. The former class of expenses is met by state appropriations and the latter by income from operations insofar as it is adequate for the purpose. Deficits have to be taken care of by legislative appropriations, with the exception of interest on revenue bonds which may be outstanding.

Table 25 shows the disbursements of state appropriations by objects of expenditures and by fiscal years beginning in 1948, when the first appropriation was made for the Authority. These expenses are those incurred by the Authority in the performance of its administrative, promotional, and developmental functions.[1]

For several years "salaries and wages" have comprised roughly two-thirds of the total expenditures of the Authority from state appropriations. The administrative personnel at the two offices and

[1] With completion of the original construction, the beginning of terminal operations, and the growth of traffic, the organization of accounts necessarily has changed. Consequently, the expense items of the earlier years are not always directly comparable as to content with those of later years. This is evident in the footnotes of Table 25.

at the two terminals, together with assistants and secretarial help, are paid from this source. On June 30, 1961, the Authority had twenty-four employees, divided as follows (see Table 26): Administration, 5; Traffic Department, 7; Operating Port—Wilmington, 7; Operating Port—Morehead City, 5.

The number of employees of the Authority at the two terminals does not include the workmen who dock ships, load, unload, move and store cargo, and perform other services. Such workers are em-

Table 25. Disbursements of State Appropriations of the North Carolina State Ports Authority by Objects of Expenditures for the Fiscal Year Ending June 30

Expense Item	1948	1949	1950	1951	1952	1953	1954
Salaries and Wages	$ 6,687	$ 28,013	$ 24,116	$ 25,848	$ 35,901	$ 54,689	$ 76,803
Supplies and Materials	228	1,140	183	300	1,225	9,514	1,326
Postage, Telephone, Telegrams	568	1,674	1,866	1,541	2,198	4,249	2,465
Travel Expense	1,261	5,508	4,312	5,567	4,785	5,472	7,580
Printing and Binding	—	—	356	62	224	297	1,816
Motor Vehicle Operation	—	413	946	865	1,327	2,575	3,561
General Expense	727	2,162	3,570	4,655	2,688	9,397	3,691
Equipment	1,474	5,011	168	1,685	2,132	11,496	3,601
Refunds	—	—	—	—	925	2,111	1,054
Additions and Betterments	—	—	—	—	—	—	5,641
Total	$ 13,445[d]	$ 43,921	$ 35,517	$ 40,523	$ 51,405	$ 99,800	$107,538
Appropriation[e]	$ 50,000	$ 50,000	$ 50,000	$ 50,000	$ 74,460	$110,060	$126,652

Expense Item	1955	1956	1957	1958	1959	1960	1961
Salaries and Wages	$ 85,491	$ 90,984	$102,617	$123,151	$130,653	$120,010	$120,598
Supplies and Materials	1,281[a]	1,849	1,900	20,097	20,100	20,094	20,100
Postage, Telephone, Telegrams	2,992[b]	4,881	5,000	7,996	8,000	7,955	8,100
Travel Expense	5,375	6,426	7,350	5,023	6,400	7,746	6,700
Printing and Binding	1,277	1,413	1,600	897	1,600	1,550	1,600
Motor Vehicle Operation	3,242	3,144	3,150	3,149	4,200	2,859	4,225
General Expense	5,604	10,628	10,900	10,679	10,900	16,828	17,000
Equipment	3,429	2,730	2,500	244	500	449	530
Refunds	—	—	—	—	—	—	—
Additions and Betterments	5,995	31,997	32,000[c]	—	—	—	—
Total	$114,686	$154,152	$167,017	$171,236	$182,353	$177,491	$178,853
Appropriation[e]	$128,052	$192,663	$194,157	$174,076	$176,427	$182,778	—

[a] $372 was for an out-of-state office.
[b] $497 was for an out-of-state office.
[c] Maintenance and repairs.
[d] Includes $2,500 of legal expense.
[e] See Table 2
Source: Biennial. Reports of the State Advisory Budget Commission.

Table 26. Distribution of the Expenses of the State Ports Authority Among the Major Classes of Expenditures[1]

	1952	1953	1954	1955	1956	1957	1958	1959	1960	1961
Administration	$ 38,960	$ 42,916	$ 48,199	$ 48,971	$ 40,429	$ 41,547	$ 43,982	$ 49,315	$ 50,142	$ 51,311
Traffic Department	7,705	16,320	20,118	47,309	50,530	62,174	64,348	66,834	61,581	61,774
Operating Port—Wilmington	1,112	30,800	16,194	16,053	34,745	34,747	36,062	36,055	36,408	36,408
Operating Port—Morehead City	2,704	20,924	16,433	16,499	28,448	28,549	26,844	30,149	29,360	29,360
Total	$ 50,481	$110,960	$100,944[a]	$128,832[b]	$154,152	$167,017	$171,236	$182,353	$177,491	$178,853

[a] There was an additional amount of $5,641 for Additions and Betterments.
[b] There was an additional amount of $6,000 for Additions and Betterments.
[1] There were the following expenditures for years prior to 1952:
 1948—Administration, $13,445.
 1949—Administration, $28,800; Traffic Department, $8,700.
 1950—Administration, $27,692; Traffic Department, $7,825.
 1951—Administration, $35,900; Traffic Department, $14,100.
Source: Biennial Reports of the State Advisory Budget Commission.

ployees of the particular terminal and not of the Authority and are
paid from operating revenue.

In the financial reports of the Authority the expenditures are
divided broadly into the following classes: Administration, Traffic

Table 27. Expenses by Classes of Items of the State Ports for the Fiscal Year
Ending June 30, 1961

Expense Item	Total	Ocean Terminals	State Docks
Operating			
Salaries—Supervisory	$ 35,684	$ 14,011	$ 21,673
Salaries—Laborers	277,600	77,279	200,321
Salaries—Watchmen	34,380	17,936	16,444
Equipment Rental	1,177	877	300
Operating Supplies	27,181	21,811	5,370
Gasoline and Oil	11,050	2,724	8,326
Insurance	25,471	5,405	20,066
Electricity	13,692	7,556	6,136
Water Purchased	6,210	3,398	2,812
Shortages and Damages	477	33	444
Heating	828	131	697
General Expense	1,944	606	1,338
Total Operating	435,694	151,767	283,927
Maintenance			
Salaries—Laborers	58,317	23,225	35,091
Supplies and Materials	25,313	12,220	13,093
Outside Repairs	5,505	1,468	4,038
Heating	742	419	323
General Expense	10	10	—
Total Maintenance	89,887	37,342	52,545
Administrative			
Salaries	64,473	30,660	33,813
Supplies and Materials	3,066	1,727	1,339
Postage	2,433	1,424	1,009
Communications Expense	4,547	1,997	2,551
Travel	5,537	2,669	2,868
Printing & Binding	5,484	2,919	2,565
Motor Vehicle Operations	2,591	1,163	1,428
Dues and Subscriptions	836	356	480
Business Promotion	4,890	2,617	2,274
Retirement Expense	4,558	2,392	2,167
Social Security Expense	13,445	4,794	8,651
Medical Insurance Expense	5,213	2,599	2,614
Interest Expense	3,702	—	3,702
Advertising	10,613	5,306	5,306
Heating	734	232	501
General Expense	20,535[a]	9,796	10,738
Total Administrative	152,657	70,651	82,006
Total Expenses	$678,238	$259,760	$418,478

[a] Includes $20,520 of non-recurring expenses.
Source: State Ports Authority, Exhibit "C".

Department, Operating Port—Wilmington, Operating Port—Morehead City.

The annual distribution among these four classes is given in Table 26. For the first four years "Administration" was the largest item of expenditure; since then the expenditure of the Traffic Department has led. Since the end of fiscal 1955, the expenditure for managing each of the ports has not fluctuated much, and neither has the expenditure of the Traffic Department since the end of fiscal 1956. The sudden jump in the expenditure for Administration in 1959 can be accounted for in the hiring of a new executive director at a considerably higher salary than his predecessor received.

Table 27 classifies and itemizes the expenditures that were made in operating the state ports for the fiscal year of 1961. This table is presented only to show the range of activities for which expenditures were made. The reader should notice that depreciation expense is not included in this table. That subject is discussed later.

In Table 27 the amount spent for labor comes to almost 70 per cent of the total expenditures. A comparison of Table 27 with Table 25 shows that the amount spent for salaries and wages to operate the ports is much more than the amount spent for the same purpose to administer them.

The individual items of expense for other years than 1961 are not included in this study, but the figures for the three broad classifications of expenses, namely, operating, maintenance, and administrative, are found in Table 30 in the section on revenue. These classes of expenses and depreciation charges are treated in the discussion of revenue and net profits.

Depreciation

The Authority has established twenty-three different classes of depreciable property at State Docks and nineteen classes at Ocean Terminals (see Table 28). The majority of the items of fixed plant are depreciated at an annual rate of 2 per cent; a few range from 4 to 6.67 per cent. Cargo-handling, maintenance, and office equipment is depreciated at rates ranging from 4 to 20 per cent, and general equipment at rates ranging from 4 to 25 per cent. Table 28 shows both the original cost of the property and the rate of depreciation.

Table 28. Depreciation Schedule of the State Ports Authority, June 30, 1961

Item	Cost	Rate (Per Cent)
Wilmington		
Wharves	$ 3,976,195	2
Dock Ramp	5,352	6⅔
Transit Shed	1,202,185	2
Storage Warehouse	1,111,503	2
Asphalt Hardstands	47,796	4
Asphalt Parking Area	6,139	4
Cargo-Handling Equipment	338,240	4-20
Two Gantry Cranes & Accessories	358,457	4
Administrative Building	102,854	2
Weighing Station	50,656	2
Fumigation Plant & Floodlights	120,960	2- 5
Garage	4,491	4
Stevedore Equipment Garage	29,746	4
Track Facilities	293,438	2
Water Tanks, Mains, & Sewers	173,402	2
Fencing, Roadways, & Pavements	113,120	2
Flagpole & Plaque	905	2
Leasehold Improvements	208,064	2
Maintenance Equipment	25,694	10-20
Office Equipment	2,360	10-20
Brick Dwelling	8,000	4
Police Office	1,520	6⅔
General Equipment	21,142	4-25
Total	$8,202,119	
Morehead City		
Wharves	$ 1,542,570	2
Wharf Repairs	24,424	20
Transit Sheds	539,300	2-2½
Storage Warehouses	1,232,021	2
Roofing Repairs	2,577	20
Cargo-Handling Equipment	186,647	10-20
Office Building	24,759	5
Fumigation Plant	153,033	2
Track Facilities	257,558	2
Roads & Pavements	251,687	2
Electrical System	18,395	2
Water Tanks, Mains, & Sewers	148,733	2
Fencing Improvements	2,782	2
Flagpole & Plaque	1,020	2
Equipment Garage	16,983	4
Maintenance Equipment	8,677	10-20
Office Equipment	3,055	10-20
Glycol Tank Improvements	5,041	10
General Equipment	16,131	6⅔-25
Total	$ 4,435,393	
Administrative		
Office Equipment	$ 10,145	6⅔
General Equipment	8,676	25
Total	18,821	
Total Fixed Assets	$12,656,433	

Source: State Ports Authority, Exhibit "E."

The total cost coincides with the figure for total depreciable properties in Table 3 (balance sheet).

Revenue

Table 29 itemizes the revenue of each of the state terminals by sources since operations began. Most of the figures for 1952 cover only a portion of the year because the facilities were opened for business only shortly before the end of the fiscal year. The items of this table indicate the kinds of work and services that are required for successful port operation.

As one would expect, a large proportion of the revenue is received from accommodating, loading, and unloading ships and storage. In its early years Ocean Terminals received substantial sums in rentals on warehouses leased to the Navy and always has received revenue for accommodating Navy vessels.

Table 30 summarizes the revenue and expense data for each of the state ports by fiscal years since operations began. Until 1956 Ocean Terminals was the more profitable port, but since then, except for 1958 when both ports operated at a loss, State Docks has returned a much higher net profit. In 1958 there was a heavy reduction in scrap iron and steel exports to foreign countries. One should recall here that at first Ocean Terminals had profitable contracts with the Navy and a general cargo terminal which the Authority had bought, whereas all the facilities had to be constructed at State Docks. Revenue began to decline at Ocean Terminals in 1955. In addition to the loss of Navy business mentioned previously, fertilizer shipments were largely abandoned, owing to the damage which these materials were causing to storage facilities.

Table 31 gives the expenses, depreciation, and net profit as a percentage of revenue for the two ports combined. The wide fluctuations for total expenses in the early years and the tendency for them to become stabilized in later years indicates an important element of constant cost in these expenses, i.e., a minimum of expenditures that must be incurred regardless of the volume of traffic.

The percentages for depreciation have declined from the levels of the earlier years and have shown a tendency to become stabilized as the ports become fully utilized. Of course, this percentage will

Table 29. Sources of Revenue from Operations of the State Ports Authority

Source of Revenue	Ocean Terminals									
	1952	1953	1954	1955	1956	1957	1958	1959	1960	1961
Wharfage	$ 37,450a	$ 54,238	$ 65,425	$ 62,969	$ 49,796	$ 35,468	$ 38,645	$ 50,249	$ 60,495	$ 70,359
Dockage	391	2,446	1,269	4,176	5,907	11,453	16,619	28,449	52,438	54,309
Handling Lines	390	560	545	1,173	2,003	2,618	3,584	5,486	7,198	8,802
Storage	50	5,116	32,972	22,357	21,131	30,046	34,713	41,295	60,931	82,057
Handling Charges	—	3,682	14,158	9,157	15,119	17,622	43,825	54,665	73,941	87,265
Equipment Rental	—	—	—	1,140	1,004	1,386	576	1,416	3,493	3,171
Other Rentals	6,238	53,129	56,347b	52,390c	26,525	14,644	5,621	9,496	14,553	17,612
Fumigation Charges	—	—	—	—	309	5,829	15,856	18,488	36,074	27,994
Weight Receipts	—	—	—	—	—	—	—	—	—	—
Thru-putd	—	—	13,545	21,240	27,007	31,324	33,638	34,347	38,154	31,814
Sale of Water	3,281	5,447	5,716e	10,933	7,099	7,312	6,706	7,785	8,971	12,246
Sale of Supplies	363	210	14,850f	2,425g	1,531	637	413	1,897	1,072	1,717
Interest Income	—	—	—	1,994	4,871	4,193	3,802	3,893	6,477	5,755
Port Magazine Income	—	—	—	958	436	716	743	859	1,167	1,475
Miscellaneous Income	—	355	545	1,351	1,209	751	1,506	2,469	1,240	2,445
Total Revenue	$ 48,163	$116,183	$205,372	$192,263	$163,947	$163,999	$206,247	$260,794	$366,604	$407,021

(Table 29 continued)

Source of Revenue	State Docks									
	1952	1953	1954	1955	1956	1957	1958	1959	1960	1961
Wharfage	$ 29,928[a]	$ 17,377	$ 14,774	$ 58,448	$ 77,773	$ 88,468	$ 66,305	$ 64,033	$112,452	$137,034
Dockage	—	411	5,029	26,770	58,788	71,057	55,830	85,792	126,184	132,024
Handling Lines	130	500	1,055	2,041	3,630	3,783	6,625	7,699	13,635	15,375
Storage	—	18,984	36,276	34,501	36,256	18,307	30,843	37,544	43,304	49,755
Handling Charges	—	54,474	48,616	84,369	100,736	106,874	143,040	181,868	261,490	224,412
Equipment Rental	2,539	6,151	—	39,403	49,038	84,241	72,585	45,096	105,909	100,554
Other Rentals	2,182	2,606	10,062[b]	7,117[a]	6,577	7,355	10,115	15,715	18,396	26,952
Fumigation Charges	—	—	—	1,440	7,427	7,004	15,363	9,024	6,429	3,821
Weight Receipts	—	109	2,548	10,838	18,655	23,475	10,466	7,898	13,130	14,735
Thru-put[d]	—	—	—	—	—	—	—	—	—	—
Sale of Water	219	998	2,213[e]	5,127	4,860	6,713	9,134	10,844	16,519	11,266
Sale of Supplies	356	1,346	—	7,531[g]	3,910	3,408	4,282	4,358	4,580	3,465
Interest Income	—	—	—	544	1,404	1,385	1,004	1,130	4,489	4,369
Port Magazine Income	—	—	—	958	435	716	743	859	1,167	1,475
Miscellaneous Income	—	2,753	4,954	557	440	680	614	450	3,383	2,223
Total Revenue	$ 35,354	$105,795	$125,527	$279,644	$369,929	$423,465	$426,949	$472,310	$731,067	$728,360

[a] Includes handling charges.
[b] Includes equipment rentals and rent of land.
[c] Includes rent of land.
[d] Revenue from running petroleum products and chemicals through pipelines and from storing these products.
[e] Includes electric current.
[f] Stevedoring.
[g] Includes sale of labor.
Source: State Ports Authority, Exhibit "C."

Table 30. Condensed Comparative Statement of Revenue and Expenses of Ocean Terminals and State Docks for the Fiscal Year Ending June 30

Ocean Terminals

Item	1952	1953	1954	1955	1956	1957	1958	1959	1960	1961
Revenue	$ 48,162	$116,184	$205,370	$192,261	$163,948	$163,999	$206,245	$260,795	$366,605	$407,020
Expenses:										
Operating	9,838	63,649	67,750	23,241	29,749	49,953	82,064	100,857	156,280	151,768
Maintenance	a	a	a	28,466	29,191	21,287	12,909	28,532	37,276	37,342
Administrative	5,711	9,290	11,754	22,530	25,119	37,450	39,799	37,198	63,090	70,651
Total	$ 15,549	$ 72,939	$ 79,504	$ 74,237	$ 84,059	$108,690	$134,772	$166,297	$256,646	$259,761
Net Profit (Loss) before Depreciation	32,613	43,245	125,866	118,024	79,889	55,309	71,473	94,498	109,959	147,259
Depreciation	—	40,590b	62,091	61,354	66,435	69,602	73,333	77,858	92,542	109,846
Net Profit (Loss)	$ 32,613	$ 2,655	$ 63,775	$ 56,670	$ 13,454c	($ 14,293)	($ 1,860)	$ 16,640	$ 17,417	$ 37,413

State Docks

Item	1952	1953	1954	1955	1956	1957	1958	1959	1960	1961
Revenue	$ 35,354	$105,795	$125,527	$279,643	$369,929	$423,465	$426,949	$472,308	$731,067	$728,360
Expenses:										
Operating	23,679	101,647	110,968	119,651	146,392	179,891	227,119	235,109	321,933	283,926
Maintenance	a	a	a	39,715	28,635	31,173	45,231	31,744	47,134	52,546
Administrative	989	51,764	18,768	22,906	28,479	43,841	46,814	40,265	67,706	82,005
Total	$ 24,668	$117,411	$129,736	$182,272	$203,506	$254,905	$319,164	$307,118	$436,773	$418,477
Net Profit (Loss) before Depreciation	10,686	(11,616)	(4,209)	97,371	166,423	168,560	107,785	165,190	294,294	309,883
Depreciation	—	60,886b	101,496	110,078	111,102	115,157	126,033	127,424	158,512	202,050
Net Profit (Loss)	$ 10,686	($ 72,502)	($105,705)	($ 12,707)	$ 55,321c	$ 53,403	($ 18,248)	$ 37,766	$135,782	$107,833

a Included in other expense categories.
b Allocated on basis of the percentages of the following few years.
c See note b, Table 31.
Source: From materials supplied by the State Ports Authority.

increase for awhile every time the plant is enlarged because the new traffic to utilize the larger plant is not usually available immediately.

In those years with a net loss, the loss was not a cash loss except in 1953 and 1954. Except for those years, the plant failed to cover depreciation charges, which are not an annual cash outlay. If these charges are covered the firm has that much more cash for use, but if they are not covered an annual outlay of cash is not involved. An examination of Table 30 will reveal that revenue has been greater than total expenses each year at Ocean Terminals and each year except 1953 and 1954 at State Docks, and even in those years at State Docks most of the loss was because of failure to cover depreciation charges. When the revenue fails to cover "total expenses," the difference must be covered by the state appropriation.

Table 32 summarizes the amounts of Table 30 for each state port and combines these into a total for both ports. By subtracting expenses from income, the net profit (or loss) will be shown in each case.

In 1955 the two ports together returned a net profit after depreciation, and in 1956, for the first time, both ports made a net profit. When the Authority was created the general belief was that eight or ten years would be required for the ports to make a net profit after operations began, and other expert estimates ranged from five to twenty years. But a profit was shown in the fourth year of operations, although losses have been incurred since that time.

In determining the net profits nothing has been allowed for the annual appropriations by the state nor for interest on the state's invest-

Table 31. Expenses and Net Profit as a Percentage of Revenue

	1952	1953	1954	1955	1956	1957	1958	1959	1960	1961
Operating Expenses	40.1	74.5	54.0	30.3	33.0	39.1	48.8	45.7	43.6	38.4
Maintenance Expenses	a	a	a	14.4	10.8	8.9	9.2	8.3	7.7	7.9
Administrative Expenses	8.3	11.3	9.2	9.6	10.0	13.9	13.7	10.5	11.9	13.4
Total Expenses	48.4	85.8	63.2	54.3	53.8	61.9	71.7	64.5	63.2	59.7
Net Profit before Depreciation	51.6	14.2	37.8	45.7	47.2	38.1	28.3	35.5	36.8	40.3
Depreciation	—	45.7	49.1	36.3	33.3	31.4	31.5	28.0	22.9	27.5
Net Profit (Loss)	—	(31.5)	(11.3)	9.4	13.9[b]	6.7	(3.2)	7.5	13.9	12.8

[a] Included in other expense categories.
[b] There was a loss of $5,204 or approximately 1 per cent of revenue on the sale of equipment.

ment of more than $12 million, although $227,927 has been paid from net profits into the State Ports Bond Sinking Fund. To June 30, 1961, the Authority had spent an aggregate amount of $1,537,937 from the annual appropriations by the state (see Table 2). The aggregate net profits to June 30, 1961, not allowing anything for depreciation for 1952, were $416,114 (see Table 30).

The management consultant firm of Cresap, McCormick, and Paget suggested recently that the ports of Georgia, South Carolina, and North Carolina consider rate increases for the use of port facilities. The firm stated that ports in these states often charge less than other ports, and often less than is needed to support the facilities. Executive Director D. Leon Williams pointed out that port officials in all three of the states were constantly aware of the need for higher rates but that the rates could not be increased beyond competitive rates farther south and along the North Atlantic coast.[2]

[2] *Durham Morning Herald*, Aug. 12, 1961, 1:3.

Table 32. Summary of Operation Income and Expenses of the State Ports for the Fiscal Year Ending June 30[1]

Year	Total		Morehead City		Wilmington	
	Income	Expenses	Income	Expenses	Income	Expenses
1952	$ 83,517	$ 40,217[a]	$ 48,162	$ 15,549[a]	$ 35,354	$ 24,668[a]
1953	221,979	291,826	116,184	113,529[b]	105,795	178,297[b]
1954	330,897	372,827	205,370	141,595	125,527	231,232
1955	471,904	427,941	192,261	135,591	279,643	292,350
1956	533,877	425,102	163,948	150,494	369,929	314,608
1957	587,464	548,354	163,999	178,292	423,465	370,062
1958	633,194	653,302	206,245	208,105	426,949	445,197
1959	733,103	678,697	260,795	244,155	472,308	434,542
1960	1,097,672	944,473	366,605	349,188	731,067	595,285
1961	1,135,380	990,134	407,020	369,607	728,360	620,527

[a] Makes no allowance for depreciation.
[b] Depreciation allocated on basis of the percentages for the following few years.
[1] Discrepancies between Table 29 and Tables 30 and 32 result from the rounding off of a large number of items in constructing Table 29.

8. Summary and Conclusions

The work of the State Ports Authority represents an attempt by the state to develop the potentialities of its economic resources more fully, thereby increasing the competitive strength of its industries. Other southeastern states (and other coastal states too) have similar organizations, some of them older and some of them younger than the State Ports Authority of North Carolina. All sections of the nation are growing industrially, some more rapidly than others. As the demand for transportation service expands there is a tendency for freight costs to increase, especially in the more heavily industrialized areas. Transportation improvements in the less congested sections may in time then provide national as well as local or regional economic benefits.

Understandably, state appropriations from the general revenues have been necessary in the early stages of the work of the State Ports Authority, but in time the port projects may be self-supporting. In the minds of some people, however, the use of state funds is justified on the ground that the improvements benefit the entire state and not just the shippers and the commercial interests at the ports.

There is a general feeling of long standing that the progress of the state has been retarded because it did not have a seaport that could handle its imports and exports. Industrial and commercial interests believe that freight rates favoring Charleston and Norfolk have retarded the growth of North Carolina seaports and that rail rates and policies which generally were unfavorable to North Carolina have slowed the growth of industry in the state. The latter condition was the underlying influence of the agitation for port development which, in turn, was to be the means for overcoming the rate disadvantages suffered by the industry and commerce of the state.

The state terminals did not begin operations until seven years after the original ports legislation was passed. At first, support for their development was not widespread, existing chiefly in the immediate port areas and on the part of a few interested people over the state. The public and the General Assembly were slow in giving their support. The public was slow in influencing the General Assembly and in using the ports after they were opened, and the General Assembly was slow in providing funds for the construction of the plant after it became evident that the use of revenue bonds was not feasible.

Recently, because the advantages of the state's modern terminals have become evident and because leading state officials have given their energetic support, there has been a growing interest in port development and expansion. State officials have been interested in an expanding state economy, as is evidenced by their efforts to attract new industries to the state, and they view modern seaports as an aid in attaining their objective.

The use of the ports after facilities had been constructed developed slowly, largely because of unfavorable or discriminatory freight rates to them. These rates have now been modified so that the ports are no longer at a competitive disadvantage in most respects, but obtaining adjustments in freight rates is a time-consuming process.

Morehead City has become one of the nation's leading tobacco-exporting ports since Ocean Terminals was opened and, given time, may develop a volume grain-exporting trade. This latter trade will be based largely on production in the state, although some midwestern grain may be attracted when the Authority decides to promote such traffic. Morehead City is also the leading point in the country for the export of fish oil, and, although this industry may grow, the tonnage will not be great. As ships arrive to load tobacco and grain there will be space on them for package cargo and this traffic, now small, may grow. Conditions are much better at Wilmington, though, for promoting traffic in package cargo. Apparently, Morehead City will be a port specializing in a few commodities.

The greater share of the tonnage at State Docks is provided by a small number of commodities, but a much larger number than at Morehead City. The important volume items are scrap metal, wood pulp, and machinery of different kinds, all export items, lumber and different manufactures made from it, iron and steel, and tools and hardware. The latter two are import items, and lumber and its manufactures are both imported and exported. The traffic in scrap metal is subject to cyclical influences. Trade in wood pulp and lumber and its manufactures should grow because of the importance of the forestry and furniture industries in the state. Traffic in machinery, iron and steel, and tools and hardware should grow as the manu-facturing industries of the state expand.

At Wilmington, the private docks and State Docks supplement each other, the former handling bulk cargo, the latter, general cargo. The possibility of obtaining high-rate general cargo is an added attraction to draw ships to the port and the possibility of obtaining space readily is an attraction for the general cargo.

The two state terminals are modern and have efficient manage-ment which gives careful attention to shipments. The management refers to this service as "personalized" service. It is a quality of service which a small, modern, growing port, operating under com-petitive conditions, can provide. Statements of many of those who have used the terminals emphasize the efficiency, speed, and care with which cargoes are handled.

When the state terminals began operations it was believed that eight or ten years would be required for them to start showing an operating profit. This goal was attained in half that time, a fact which speaks well for the policies of the responsible state officials and of the Authority and for the capabilities of the administrative per-sonnel.

The state ports are subsidized to the extent that revenues fail to cover the sum of the annual state appropriations for administrative purposes and the annual charges on the state's investment. To June 30, 1961, the Authority had spent an aggregate amount of $1,537,937 from the annual state appropriations. The aggregate net operating profits to June 30, 1961, were $416,114, leaving a difference of $1,121,823, which has been contributed by the taxpayer for admin-istration, promotion, and operations. An additional cost is the annual interest charge on the state's investment. A portion of this amount consists of the interest paid on port bonds of the original issue still outstanding. The interest on the remaining amount of the investment does not involve an annual payment by the state since this investment was made from appropriations for capital improve-ments, but there is the annual economic cost for the amount of pro-ductive resources employed.

The fact of the subsidy does not necessarily mean that the resources involved are being used without their making any economic return. Furthermore, even though these productive resources may be employed inefficiently at present, in time, as port operations gain momentum, the state ports may become self-supporting.

The State Ports Authority has done well in the time that it has operated, and there does not seem to be any reason why the commerce at the two state ports should not continue to increase gradually if the present policies are continued. But the kinds of activities in which the Authority is engaged are highly competitive. It is not easy to uproot traffic from established channels. Potential customers must be convinced of the long-range benefits of making a change. The Authority now has efficiently-operated modern terminals which should generate momentum. But it also is necessary to have a permanent program for keeping present and potential customers informed about the services which the ports have to offer and for informing the public about the economic advantages of the ports to the state. The Authority has gradually developed a program of this kind.

Index